Contents

Writing matters

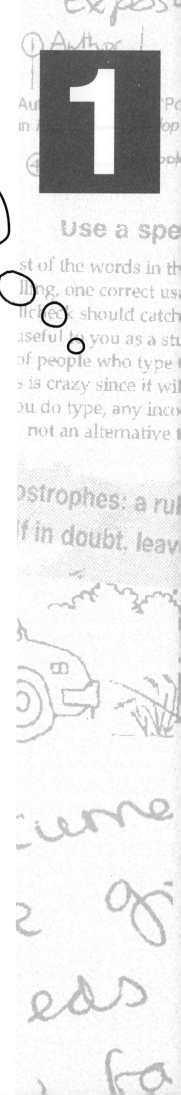

> No,
> I don't mark students on their writing.
> But, you know, there is a remarkable correlation between
> the students who do write well and the higher grades at the
> end of the day – about 100 per cent I'd say.
>
> (Computing lecturer)

Whatever your subject, you need to be able to write well. In some arts and humanities subjects this is obvious; if the subject matter is words, it stands to reason that your ability to write well is crucial to your success. But computing? Engineering? If the program works or the bridge stays up, is that not enough?

The answer is 'no'. In these subjects too you need to be able to record your actions, explain your thoughts, and demonstrate your understanding in a reader-friendly way. The difference is that it may not be an explicit requirement. Take another look at the hidden messages in the computing lecturer's comment: you are not marked up or down on the quality of your writing; however, people who get higher grades write well – or is it that people who write well get higher grades?

However you look at it, the link between thinking, writing and academic success is clear. In some courses, the ability to write well is an explicit requirement, reflected in the assessment criteria – you gain or lose marks depending on the quality of your writing. In others it is implicit; you get the odd scrawled comment in the margin about accuracy, but there doesn't appear to be any direct connection with the grade. As a student, this leaves you with the problem of what to do about the feedback. It is clear, from comments by tutors and students, that both parties feel there is a core of basic writing skills that is not taught in higher education, and often has not been acquired earlier in the student's career.

This series of Student Guides, 'Developing Writing', is designed to bridge that gap. The other guides are about how to write well using the particular forms, structures and conventions of academic writing – reports, essays and so on. This guide is about how to respond to a type of comment found on students' work in all subject areas:

'Write shorter sentences.'

'Sentence construction sometimes weak – need to ensure sense is clear.'

'Need to pay more attention to writing coherent paragraphs.'

'What is this last paragraph about?'

'Cite references properly.'

These comments are about how, as a writer, you convey your message to your reader and achieve your purpose in writing. To do this effectively, you need to be able to work the conventions of academic writing. There are rules for this game as for any other: the conventions of sentence and paragraph structure, and the basics of grammar and expression.

1.1 How to use this guide

You will see from the Contents page that this guide has a lot of short chapters. This is to enable you to identify what you need to work on and find the relevant section easily. Each chapter is self-contained, with simple explanations and material to work on to help you develop skills in each area. You will also find a lot of cross-referencing to other sections in the guide. This is a way of providing additional material for you to think about and work on when you feel that reinforcement is necessary. The extracts in the appendix are for use in this way. They are employed for several activities in the guide.

How you use this guide is up to you. You may want to work on the quick reference sections, and note the longer activities to come back to another time. When you do decide to undertake a longer activity, do commit the time to work through it before you check with the answer section. You learn much better by doing . . .

Strategic thinking

The detail of how you write is derived from the context in which you write. The starting point for this guide, as for the others in the series, is to think about some key issues before you set out on a writing task.

2.1 Ask key questions

- **What?**

- **Why?**

- **Who?**

Before you start working, and certainly before you start writing, you need to be absolutely clear about what you are aiming to achieve. With any writing task, it helps to start with some prompt questions. The first set helps to clarify the task itself:

- **What** exactly do I have to produce? What content? What form? What guidance do I have about this?

- **Why** am I writing this? What do you want to put across? What does your reader want to get out of it? What is your purpose?

- **Who** is it for? What are the needs and expectations of your actual audience: the tutor (which tutor?), the seminar/workshop group? The hypothetical audience: the assignment scenario?

Your answers to these questions will take you to the purpose of your writing, give you a clear idea of the needs of your reader or audience, and from there bring you to the form and style of the finished piece.

In approaching a writing task in this way, you are in good company.

Before you begin to write make sure that you:

YOU MUST KNOW

- *your subject*

- *your reason for writing*

- *your reader*

a) have a clear understanding of your subject

b) know why you are writing – what does your correspondent want to know and why does he want to know it?

c) adapt your style and the content of the letter or minute to suit your correspondent's needs and their present knowledge of the subject.

YOU MUST BE

- *clear*

- *simple and brief*

- *accurate and complete*

- *polite and human.*

This advice was first published in 1948, by Sir Ernest Gowers in his *Plain Words*. The prime audience for his advice was a bureaucratic and pompous civil service in the 1940s. He then suggests that his readers use these points as a checklist: is it clear? simple and brief? accurate? complete? human? These are useful headings for any checklist.

Once you have clarified the key points about the context in which you are writing, you can move on to the second set of key questions. These help you to establish a sensible programme of work within the constraints of deadlines, working methods, people available, equipment and so on.

- **How** do I do this?

- **When** do I carry out the work? The write-up?

- **Where** does the work need to be done?

Most guidance on writing skills is about the question **how**? This guide is no exception. The pages that follow are all about *how*: how to use apostrophes, commas, semi-colons, colons; how to write sentences and paragraphs; how to record and present your sources; and so on. This guide also touches on the question why? It is worth remembering that the question how? came fourth in the list of key questions here. Only after you have clarified your answers to the first three key questions does the question how? have any relevance. When you can see the form, the purpose and the audience of your task, you can then work on how to achieve your objectives through the detail of your writing.

There are not that many fixed rights and wrongs in writing that hold good for all time in all contexts. What matters is to be able to choose the right style for the occasion, and to adapt your style to the different contexts in which you write.

The extracts below show this process at work.

The following notes were written in a student's fieldwork log:

> Location 5 SHEEP'STOR GRAVEL PIT
> Grid ref: SX 5568 6792
>
> Exposed bedrock – extremely decomposed granite.
> Strong yellow / brown / orange in colour which
> crumbles easily in fingers. Possibly mechanical
> weathering too.
> Grown – coarse crystalline texture of granite
> parent rock which breaks down into individual
> mineral grains in the hand.
>
> Location 6 FOOT OF SHEEP'S TOR
> Grid ref: SX 5605 6810
> Gained to the top.
> Rest of day spent struggling against wind,
> rain, cold and hunger and exhaustion . . .
> Don't really have much on this site as
> everyone was fed up, tired, wet etc ..

From logs by Rosie Sutherland and Kirstin Whittingham

The log was written in pencil, hard to decipher in places, and petered out when the elements became too extreme. If the students had tried to rewrite their logs, or smarten them up, they would have been heavily penalized, as the tutor's guidance makes clear.

Developing Writing – Essential Writing Skills

Below is an extract from the written acccount produced by this group of students some time later:

> Today the main processes of erosion are not those caused by the physical processes of fluvial abrasion and attrition, but by mechanical and chemical processes. One of the most striking features of the granite scenery in the south-west is that of the tors. These have been formed by a combination of chemical weathering, exploiting the jointing system of the granite below the surface, and through the action of the freeze thaw . . .

From an essay *The Environment Impact of Granite on the South-West of England*. These extracts are also considered in Student Guide 3: *Scientific and Technical Writing*, Section 4.1.

Gone is the feeling of exposure to the elements of Dartmoor, and in its place is a calm account of the the current processes of erosion. The final essay, as you can see, is fluent, thoughtful and well presented. If the writers had not worked on this piece of writing, drafting and redrafting, they would have been penalized. The language and style of each extract is wholly appropriate to the purpose for which it was written.

The point to take away from this is that questions of right and wrong in writing, correct and incorrect, are primarily to do with what is appropriate to your present purpose. That said, you need to develop the full range of writing skills, so you have the choice of changing your style from one occasion to the next. This is where advice on 'How to . . .' comes into its own. Use it selectively to help you develop this range.

2.2 Judging the context

The extracts in the appendix are taken from a range of sources typical of those to be found in student folders on any campus or on the shelves of any university library.

Activity

Read the extracts and make notes on them under the headings in the grid below. Feedback on this activity is in the appendix.

- **Source** – what sort of text do you think the extract is taken from?
- **Audience** – what can you deduce about the intended audience?
- **Evidence** – what led you to form your view?
- **Purpose** – what do you think each writer was trying to achieve? How successful do you think each has been?

Extract	Source	Audience	Evidence	Purpose
A				
B				
C				
D				
E				
F				
G				

Glimpsing the process

You know from your own experience that writing is a process, often a chaotic, frustrating and depressing one, as you struggle towards a final form. You also know that your reader, quite rightly, will have certain expectations of the end-product. She or he will be looking for a piece that conforms to certain norms, with a certain appearance, length and language, and an arrangement of material with a beginning, a middle and an end. Although it may not seem so at the time, the processes you go through as you work towards the end product do, nevertheless, have some kind of sequence in time and phasing.

Each student guide in the series considers the processes that underpin each form of writing (working with data, a report, an essay). Below, the processes that are common to all writing tasks are shown in bold. These are the ones outlined in this chapter.

The process of writing

- **Gathering information**

  Distilling ideas – getting something on paper

  Planning your work

- **Writing the first draft**

  Reviewing and editing

  Writing the final draft

- **Presenting your work**

3.1 Gathering information

At different times you will draw on all sorts of different sources for your work. Many of your sources will be printed, because this is how you gain access to what other people in your field have done and thought. Chapter 9 considers this process in greater detail.

Record your sources meticulously, so you know where ideas and studies come from. If you don't you may

- have to retrace your steps later – very annoying and time consuming

- not get the credit for the work you have done

- not realize you are plagiarizing, and use other people's ideas without acknowledging them.

You need to record the seven points of information (where applicable) shown below as the basis for an accurate bibliography.

Record these details from your reading (seven points)

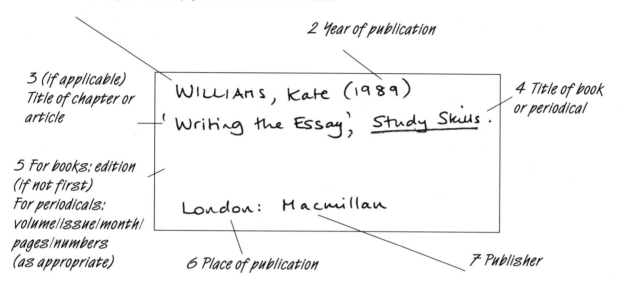

1 Author(s) or editor(s): surname and initials

2 Year of publication

3 (if applicable) Title of chapter or article

4 Title of book or periodical

WILLIAMS, Kate (1989)
' Writing the Essay', <u>Study Skills</u> .

5 For books: edition (if not first) For periodicals: volume/issue/month/ pages/numbers (as appropriate)

London: Macmillan

6 Place of publication

7 Publisher

For your references in your bibliography:

Williams, K. (1989) 'Writing the Essay', *Study Skills.* London: Macmillan.

If you note the details as you go, you will have everything you need to put together your bibliography when your deadline looms.

3.2 Writing the first draft

What's the difference between a practised or a professional writer and an occasional or a student writer? The key distinction is probably the amount of work professional writers put in between the first and the final draft. Good writers polish and edit ruthlessly, pruning redundant words and phrases, looking at what they have written from several angles, to make sure the meaning will be clear to all their intended readers. Less practised writers often hand in the first draft of what they have written, with all the uncertainties and inaccuracies there on the page, obstacles in the way of the reader.

How do you react to the following piece of writing?

> With the onset of the nineteenth century, towns and cities expanded outwards and some more than others, mainly the industrial orientated areas, many new production methods were being created and were being aided by the growth of the railways. Also in the meantime the population was rapidly growing, 40% growth in a decade in most large cities was the norm, so new developments had to be be met to accommodate the demand, most places adapted to their geographical locations so some areas grew quicker than some.

You probably feel that this is not reader-friendly writing. Has the writer read what he or she has written? As a reader, you can see how distracting and annoying it is to have to do the basic copy-editing the writer should have done. It is not the reader's job to have to puzzle out the writer's meaning. This reader – the tutor – was most restrained, and wrote

'I think you ought to write shorter sentences.'

This is a polite way of saying

- what exactly are you trying to say? If you are not clear how am I supposed to know?

- rephrase, prune and rewrite. Take one point at a time, and write a short sentence for each.

Activity: Drafting and redrafting

Edit and rewrite the extract above to make the writer's meaning clear to you. Cut out unnecessary words, write short sentences, and reword where you need to. When you have done this, compare your version with mine in the feedback section at the end of the chapter.

3.3 Presenting your work

First impressions

Readers' impressions form quickly. As a reader, you start to form impressions from the moment you handle a text, well before you settle down to decipher the words. If, as a writer, you give a bad first impression, it is much harder to make up the ground with the brilliance of your content later. The writer of the extract above is now at a real disadvantage with us, the readers. Equally, if you give a good first impression, the tutor – or external examiner – approaches your work positively, expecting it to be good as well as look good.

- Is this going to be easy to read? Clear handwriting, good clear type? Or illegible handwriting, faint, single-line spacing?

- Does it look as if the writer knows where they are going? Does the layout suggest a clear organization or argument? Or are paragraphs/sections long and rambling or short and poorly developed?

- Is this going to be hard to follow, with distracting inaccuracies in spelling and punctuation? Or is the writer in control?

Writing a good introduction is also an aspect of creating a good first impression. See Student Guide 5: *Writing Essays*, Section 5.2, for work on this.

The final product

Make sure you know what the specific requirements are, and which aspects of presentation you can decide for yourself. Here are some prompts.

Format

- Will you have a title page? Headings and sub-headings or continuous prose?

- Will you include data or diagrams? What are the requirements for these? What goes in the text, and what in the appendix?

- Have you kept records of sources consulted for the bibliography? How will you secure your work? Folder? Staple?

- Have your included the administrative details? Self-assessment sheets, if required, paperwork?

Handwritten work

- Is your writing easy to read? If in doubt show a sample to a couple of friends you trust to give an honest (but not lugubrious) comment on its readability. If they have problems

  - try writing bigger/smaller. Standard-sized writing of eight to ten words per line tends to be easier to read than very large or very small writing.

  - Concentrate on the formation of three or four problematic letters.

Word-processed work

- Use double or one and a half spacing. Your work is intended to be interactive with your tutor/reader, so leave space for comments.

- Leave a wide margin for comments, and so that any binding does not obscure your text.

- Check your print is dark and clear.

- Use the spellcheck, and scrutinize for errors the spellcheck will miss (see Section 8.9 below).

Check carefully for avoidable errors

  - especially those that come in the impression management category.

This chapter has been designed to give you a brief overview of some of the processes you go through when you write. I hope, too, that you are convinced that you – like every other writer – need to work on the detail of your writing until it does the job you want it to. The following chapters give you the tools for the job.

3.4 Feedback on activities

3.2: Drafting and redrafting: Activity

You may have produced something like this:

At the beginning of the nineteenth century, towns and cities expanded outwards, especially those in industrial areas. New production methods were being introduced, aided by the growth of the railways. The population in most large cities grew rapidly, by 40% in a decade, and housing had to be built for this increased population.

There is an element of guesswork in editing what someone else has written. The author may feel that I have misrepresented what she or he was trying to say. Perhaps they meant 'created'? Perhaps the repetition about some areas expanding more than others was intended? When it is your work, however, you know what you want to say. Make sure you say it.

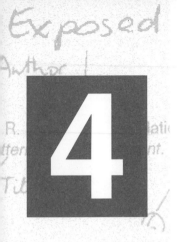
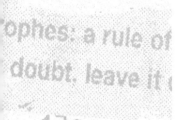
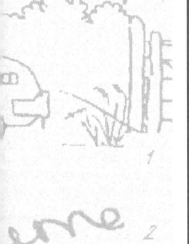

Using apostrophes

You are the reader. How do you react to the following piece of writing?

> The company needs to consider the impact of its system for sales quota's and bonuses on the motivation of the sales team. Is it practical or beneficial to the business if it is viewed by its customers as having unethical and questionable sales tactics to gain a competitive edge? The company must take opportunity's like this to make the point forcefully to its sales force. The whole organisation and its corporate responsibility to its customers could be irreparably damaged if this sales tactics are allowed to continue.

The tutor found the errors in this extract so distracting that she was only dimly aware of its content. She awarded a low grade. As reader, were you similarly distracted?

Look again: all the errors bar one are are result of the writer misusing one piece of punctuation – the apostrophe. This is, happily, the easiest piece of punctuation to learn to use correctly.

4.1 The rules

Apostrophes have two uses only

1   To mark missing letters

- He'll wait   =   he will wait

- It's Monday   =   it is Monday

- They didn't think   =   they did not think

In academic writing, you will not normally use these forms – you will write more formally, in full.

2   To show belonging – the possessive

i)   Where something belongs to one person or thing, use 's:

- She waited for ages outside the lecturer's room.
- Hockey's comments on the relevance of science to nursing are widely seen as . . .
- Write up your notes from today's seminar.
- England's aristocracy saw little change in the period 1750 to 1850.

ii)   Where something belongs to more than one, add an apostrophe to the plural, or 's to the plural form of the word.

- She waited for ages outside the lecturers' room. (Two or more lecturers share a room.)

- The European currencies' failure to stabilize under the ERM   . . .

- The children's responses to the questionnaire indicated that the 'fitfreaks' also ate a more healthy diet.

Note these uses

1

- `She was offered an afternoon's work.`
- `The department is five minutes' walk from the canteen.`

In these examples, the apostrophe is a form of the possessive; it is a shorthand for 'worth' or 'lasting'. If in doubt, pause and think about the meaning.

2

People often put apostrophes with dates, but these are not necessary.

- `The 1980s saw the rise of the yuppy.`
- `1960s fashions made a come-back.`

The rogue apostrophe – it's time for a word about its use.

Rogue 1

Take a good look at the above heading. 'Its' has two meanings, and only one has an apostrophe:

- it's time = it is time (missing letter). Use an apostrophe.

- its use = belongs to (possessive). Never use an apostrophe.

The only time you use an apostrophe with 'its' is when it means 'it is'. Since it's unlikely that you'll often find yourself writing in this chatty style, it's probably fair to say **don't use an apostrophe when you write 'its'.**

Rogue 2

Never use an apostrophe just because you have a plural:

>one tutor/two tutors;

>one quota/two quotas;

>one opportunity/two opportunities.

And that's it! There really are no exceptions to these two straightforward rules for using apostrophes.

> ## Apostrophes: a rule of thumb
> ## If in doubt, leave it out.

Try it. It's usually right.

4.2   Try it out

This section takes the form of three activities on identifying correct and incorrect uses of the apostrophe. Do them when you are ready to. When you have had a go, check your reactions with mine in the feedback section at the end of the chapter.

Activity 1: Students' writing

Below are some extracts from students' writing. Read them quickly and for each one decide

- whether apostrophes are used correctly and appropriately

- whether any apostrophes are missing.

In each case be clear about your reasons.

a   Our mistakes taught us quickly about the design process and it's implications.

b   Roy believes that ones adaptive level is controlled by three sets of stimuli.

c   The larger conurbation's experienced higher than average unemployment.

d   The General Manager has demanded an explanation and Mr Wilson's reply has been received by his direct superior.

e   The flood warning wasn't as effective as it should have been because the council officers didn't act quickly enough.

f   Our groups bridge was placed on the two tables and the bricks lowered gently.

g   It's probably fair to say that the French population's inherent nationalism would favour this overseas production.

h   It's aim was to help to alleviate the problems caused by the fixed and floating exchange rates.

i   Englands countryside was its main source of concern.

j   The computer consults it's database and either asks for more information or give's its opinion.

Activity 2: The company needs to consider . . .

Look back to the extract at the beginning of this chapter (*The company needs to consider . . .*) and correct the errors.

Activity 3: Looking at writing

Look at the extracts A–G in the appendix. Ring all the apostrophes, and see if you can explain why each is used.

4.3 Feedback on activities

Activity 1: Students' writing

a) Wrong. It should be **its implications** (possessive).

b) Wrong. It should be **one's adaptive level . . .** (possessive).

c) Wrong. 'Conurbations' is simply a plural – **conurbation** with an 's' on the end.

d) Correct. **Mr Wilson's reply** (possessive).

e) Correct but inappropriate in academic writing. It should be **was not**, **did not**.

f) Wrong. Apostrophe needed in **our group's bridge** (possessive).

g) 'It's' = it is. Correct but inappropriate. Write 'it is'.

   population's is correct (possessive).

h) Wrong. It should be **Its aim** (possessive), no apostrophe.

i) Should be **England's** – possessive; **its** is correct.

j) Wrong. **It's database** should be **its database** (possessive);

   give's – a case of scattering apostrophes whenever you see an 's'.

   Correct. **Its opinion** (possessive).

Activity 2: The company needs to consider . . .

The company needs to consider the impact of its system for sales quotas and bonuses on the motivation of the sales team. Is it practical or beneficial to the business if it is viewed by its customers as having unethical and questionable sales tactics to gain a competitive edge? The company must take opportunities like this to make the point forcefully to its sales force. The whole organization and its corporate responsibility to its customers could be irreparably damaged if these sales tactics are allowed to continue.

This was a straightforward editing job – simply a matter of taking out all the apostrophes and making two small changes: *opportunity's* to *opportunities*, and *this sales* to *these sales*.

Activity 3: Looking at writing

Extract C has four apostrophes:

decision-makers' own schooling (possessive); *decision-makers' children* (possessive); *children's education* (possessive); *parents' decisions* (possessive).

Extract D has one: *Einstein's equations* (possessive).

None of the others has any. You can see from this that

1 the possessive is effectively the only use of the apostrophe in academic writing – and the only one you need bother about.

2 It is worth noting how rarely the apostrophe is used in this sample of writing styles. If you find yourself peppering your work with apostrophes, you are probably misusing them.

Remember: if in doubt,
leave it out!

5 Writing sentences

Sense?
Sentence?
This is not a sentence – it does not make sense!

These are the sorts of comments that tell you your reader (only a tutor would actually say this) is having problems in following your flow of thought. It also tells you that the problem lies in how you construct sentences. The simple answer is to write shorter sentences. If you can do this, go ahead, and your problem is resolved. The trouble is that, if you do not know what a sentence is, you are probably not much the wiser when your reader scrawls comments like these!

There are no easy answers to this. Your best bet is to come at the question from as many angles as you can. This chapter aims to help in this by

1   looking closely at extracts from other people's writing to see how they construct sentences

2   thinking about the dictionary definition

3   considering the grammatical explanation

4   practising on other people's writing. Here we use prose that needs editing, and an extract that is well written but with punctuation removed.

5.1   Full stops and sentences

The full stop is the most important piece of punctuation because it divides writing into sentences, the basic unit of sense. That said, don't feel that short, simple sentences suggest that you are a simple thinker. It is much harder to write short simple sentences about complex matters than to write long rambling ones, adding on bits attached by commas as you gallop along trying to catch up with your thoughts.

> ### Activity: Looking at writing
>
> Look at the extracts from the essay (F) and research paper (C) in the appendix. Ring all the punctuation used.
>
> - What punctuation is used?
> - What is the average length of the sentences in each extract?
> - Which extract do you find easier to read? Why?

'Write shorter sentences'

If tutors make this comment on your work, do just this.

- Keep most sentences **under 20 words**.
- **Don't** let your sentences **go above 30 words**.

This is so you can

- think clearly
- express yourself clearly
- be reader-friendly.

5.2 What is a sentence?

You probably know this already. At least, you know what a sentence isn't. You read what you have written, and something is left hanging. It doesn't quite say what you wanted it to . . . This gut feeling about what is or is not right is all you need to write well. If you do not have this intuitive grasp, however, then you need to try and develop it by other means – such as the explanations in sections 5.2 and 5.3. If this is not for you, skip it. It is only useful if you find it so.

If you are having problems in defining a sentence, you are in good company:

> A sentence is not easy to define. Many learned grammarians have tried, and their definitions have been torn in pieces by other learned grammarians. (*Gowers, 1948*)

The dictionary at least gives a definition:

> A series of words in connected speech or writing, forming the grammatically complete expression of a single thought: . . . such a portion of a composition or utterance as extends from one full stop to another. (*Shorter Oxford Dictionary*)

Central to the dictionary definition is the idea of the sentence as a unit of sense, 'a single thought'. A full stop, it tells us, shows where each thought ends.

5.3 The grammatical approach

Grammar has added some specific guidelines to the dictionary definition: a sentence must have a main clause – a core statement, however short, that makes sense on its own. To this core statement, other phrases and clauses can be added. Punctuation within the sentence gives your writing the structure that pauses and intonation give to your speech.

The difficulty, of course, lies in getting this right in practice. How short can a sentence be? Do you look silly writing short sentences when academic journals are full of long ones? To find out the options open to you, look closely at the decisions on punctuation and style other writers have made.

Activity: How short is a short sentence?

It varies. (That is a sentence. So is this.)

Have a look at the extracts in the appendix.

- Underline the shortest sentence in each extract.
- Note in pencil the number of words in each sentence.
- Ring any additional punctuation used in these sentences.
- As you go, see if you can identify the core statement in each sentence.

The shortest sentences from some of the extracts are listed below, with the core statement ('main clause') highlighted in italics. Some are very short; others have phrases which add detail to some aspect of the core statement. The grammatical test of a full sentence is that you should be able to answer the following two questions from within it:

Question 1: **Who** or **wha**t is this sentence about?

Question 2: This (who or what) **does what**?

The answers to these will lead you back to the core statement – if you have a full sentence. See how this works with the shortest sentences from the first two extracts below.

Extract A

A ceasefire around the city *is holding.*

Q1 Who or what is this sentence about?

A *A ceasefire*

Q2 A ceasefire does what?

A *is holding.*

Extract B

Heat reaches the cooler end by conduction through the material of the rod.

Q1 Who or what is this sentence about?

A *Heat*

Q2 Heat does what?

A *reaches the cooler end.*

Activity: Grammar buff

Try the same exercise on some of the other sentences.

Extract E

Work in pairs.

Q1   Who or what is this sentence about?

A _____

Q2   You do what?

A _____

Extract F

The inner cities, with their inherent social, economic and physical problems, *provided an ideal opportunity for local authority planners to employ these powers.*

Q1   Who or what is this sentence about?

A _____

Q2   . . . do what?

A _____

Extract G

In addition to the processes identified by dual and radical theories, *workers themselves have contributed to segmentation.*

Q1   Who or what is this sentence about?

A _____

Q2   . . . do what?

A _____

What matters is that you should be able to identify a sentence, and edit and rework what you have written so your writing is in full, clear, short sentences. If the grammar helps, great, if not, try another approach.

5.4   Editing other people's writing

This is no substitute for working on your own writing, but it is useful experience. It is often easier to see other people's mistakes than it is to see your own – which is why it is a good idea to get someone else to look at your work.

Activity: Editing and rewriting

Rephrase, punctuate and cut out unnecessary words from the extract below to make the writer's meaning clear to you, the reader. Keep your changes to the minimum necessary for clarity. Aim for short sentences. Only allow yourself one sentence that goes over 20 words.

Caring for the patient does not stop at the bedside of the patient the family has to be considered, if a patient were to die the nurse would have to draw on her sociological, psychological and biological knowledge in order to comfort the family explaining why death occurred and understanding what the family are going through after the death the nurse draws on the sociological knowledge, so as to counsel the family who almost become the patient, the nurse may even disclose personal experiences to the family showing the tragedy happens to everyone, as a social worker would do when counselling this disclosure of personal experiences breaks down a wall between two relative strangers building up trust.

5.5   Review

Look back to the dictionary definition of a sentence in Section 5.2. The elements of this definition should make more sense now.

A sentence is:

> 'a series of words in connected speech or writing'

This takes us back to what writing is all about – the link between thought and the written word. You need to know what you want to say before you can say it.

> 'a single thought'

The thought can be long or short – even very short. The more bits there are to the thought, the longer the sentence, and the more careful you have to be to mark the sections with correct punctuation. The best advice is to keep your sentences short.

> 'between one full stop and another'

- A sentence ends with a full stop.

- Question marks and exclamation marks include a full stop in their design (??? !!!). They serve the same purpose.

You will rarely, if ever, need to use an exclamation mark in academic writing.

These are the basics, and you have to apply them to your own work.

- Read your own work critically at the drafting stage, well before you hand it in. Make sure each statement makes sense to you, and connects with what went before and what comes after. Then show it to someone you trust. If it makes sense to them, you've cracked it. Rewrite and celebrate.

- Develop your own awareness of how other people write. Try stopping over one paragraph in the course of a reading session, and see if you can explain why the the words between two full stops are a sentence. You will probably soon find examples of published writing that breaks all the rules . . .

5.6 Feedback on activities

5.1: Looking at writing: Activity

Extract C The writer uses no punctuation at all within the sentences, and relies on a simple structure and clear organization to carry the reader through. The writer is addressing a well defined specialist audience, and assumes that intended readers will give the abstract close attention because they will be deciding whether to commit time to reading the whole paper. With an average of 26 words, sentences are long but would generally be considered an acceptable length for a research paper abstract.

Extract F is a very readable piece. The reader – a tutor or fellow student – will be able to follow the argument of the essay with ease. The sentences are short, averaging 19 words, and the careful use of commas in the third sentence stops it from being dull. This essay was graded as a first.

5.3 Grammar buff: Activity

If you have something along these lines, you are well on the way to becoming a grammar buff.

Extract E

Work in pairs.

Q   Who or what is this sentence about?

A   *You.* (This is understood. The writer is addressing you, the reader, with an instruction.)

Q   You do what?

A   *Work in pairs.*

Extract F

The inner cities, with their inherent social, economic and physical problems, *provided an ideal opportunity* for local authority planners to employ these powers.

Q1 Who or what is this sentence about?

A   *The inner cities*

Q2 The inner cities do what?

A   *. . . provide an ideal opportunity for . . .*

Extract G

In addition to the processes identified by dual and radical theories, *workers themselves have contributed to segmentation.*

Q1 Who or what is this sentence about?

A *workers*

Q2 Workers do what?

A *have contributed to . . .*

5.4: Editing and rewriting: Activity

You may end up with something like this:

Caring for the patient does not stop at the bedside of the individual patient. The family has to be considered. When a patient dies, the nurse draws on her specialist knowledge in order to comfort the family. The nurse has to explain why death occurred and try to understand what the family are going through. After the death, the nurse needs to draw on sociological knowledge to counsel the family. The nurse may even disclose personal experiences to the family to show that tragedy happens to everyone, as a social worker would do. This disclosure of personal experiences breaks down a wall between two relative strangers and helps to build up trust.

It is still not brilliant writing, but it does make sense!

Writing complex sentences

Writing long and complex sentences is a risky business. The longer your sentence, the greater the chance that you will get lost in it somewhere and place unnecessary obstacles in the way of your reader. That said, you will, of course, want to write longer sentences, to introduce variety to your writing. That's fine – but make sure you get it right. If you are stuck, you always have an acceptable alternative – writing short sentences.

These are the tools of the trade in writing longer sentences.

- Be clear about what you want to say. Get your thoughts in order, and use simple, clear language.

- Use commas correctly.

- Colons and semi-colons are optional extras. Use them only if you know what you are doing and why you are doing it.

6.1 Using commas

Never use a comma instead of a full stop.
Write short sentences instead.

Commas have two main uses, which are definite enough to be called 'rules':

1 between items in lists

2 round a non-essential phrase or sub-clause.

Look closely at the way commas are used in the examples below.

1 Between items in a list

    Notions of rent, capital and land ownership were central to
    the writings of Karl Marx.

    The report should be made by the injured person, the First
    Aider concerned, or the Manager to whom the accident is
    first reported.

Note that 'or' linking the last two items often takes the place of a comma. The same applies to 'and' used in this way.

2 Round a sub-clause:

Commas mark off a word, phrase or clause that is not absolutely essential to the sentence.

Three specific uses (2A, 2B and 2C) are detailed below.

6.2 Commas for clauses

The use of commas in lists, whether the list is of single words or phrases, is straightforward. The use of commas in clauses, however, needs more work. This is because, if you don't know how to use commas in this way, or understand why they are used when you see them, it is all too easy to feel that you can pop in a comma when you feel like resting your pen. This plays havoc with your sentence structure and your meaning.

This section goes into some detail on the use of commas with clauses. Work through it when you are ready. At the end of it, you should be able to explain the use of every comma you see!

2A   A single comma is used when the word, phrase or clause comes first or last.

Study the examples below to see how this works.

Word

Here, the implications for implementing health-related exercise and physical education are more or less straightforward.

Phrase

In practice, the argument of monopoly powers being used to determine prices is difficult to sustain in the market for new houses.

There is greater emphasis on health-related behaviours, in the use of tobacco and drugs, *for example*.

Clause

Although it cannot be guaranteed that the newly created jobs will be taken by local residents, the scheme creates interest in previously under-used areas.

The major evaluation instrument was the pupil's questionnaire, *which aimed to measure aspects of a healthy lifestyle*.

Note . . .

When the phrase comes at the beginning of the sentence (like this), you need a comma.

. . . But

You don't need a comma when the main clause comes first (like this).

2B   A pair of commas is used when the non-essential word, phrase or clause comes in the middle of a sentence.

Word

It was cotton, *however*, which was the cornerstone of industrial change in England.

Phrase

Physical education, *using movement as its medium of learning and expression*, is an integral part of the education process.

Major infrastructure projects, *both motorways and airports*, were sanctioned by central government.

Clause

It would appear that primary-school girls, *if they are given the opportunity*, are just as motivated and keen to take part in exercise and sport as their male counterparts.

Enclosure, *which affected nearly one-fifth of England's arable land*, was concentrated in the east of the country.

This sentence structure is little used by students, perhaps because you have to break the thought in the main clause to add in the non-essential phrase – and then remember to conclude the thought. Try it: it is a good idea to be able to use a variety of constructions.

2C   Commas are used to mark off direct speech from what comes before or after it.

> In effect, this use of commas, in pairs or singly as appropriate, is just an extension of the use of the comma to mark sub-clauses.
>
> 'I'd love to ring your tutor', said John Patten, Secretary of State for Education, 'and get a reading of *your* intellectual capacity.'
>
> (The reply by John Patten, then Secretary of State for Education, to an Oxford student, who had asked a question about an apparent contradiction in two statements by John Major. Fran Abrams, *Independent on Sunday*, 20 March 1994)

These are the rules for using commas. You will find that experienced writers develop their own ways of using commas, some correct, some incorrect. A useful way of seeing how these rules are applied and adapted is to stop for a few moments when you are reading, and see if you can explain each piece of punctuation in one paragraph.

Activity: Comma watch

1   Turn to Extract A in the appendix. Ring all the commas and number them sequentially. See if you can explain why each is used. Check with my comments in the feedback section at the end of this chapter.

2   Do the same for Extracts F and G.
     It gets harder when you find several uses of the comma, apparently running into one another, all in the same sentence. However, the reasons for use still apply. Have a go at this.

3   Look at Extract D. Ring and number the commas down to ' . . . have forgotten' – 13 in all. Again, see if you can explain why each is used.

You do not need complex punctuation to write well. You do, however, need to

*   know what you want to say

*   remember that you are writing for a reader, so be courteous, and minimize distracting and avoidable errors

*   use clear, simple wording, and short sentences.

And, if and when you do decide to use longer sentences, use commas correctly, in order to guide your reader through.

6.3   Developing a range: semi-colons and colons

You will have noticed the occasional use of semi-colons and colons in this guide, and in other things that you read. Semi-colons and colons can be useful in showing links between ideas, and so help your reader to anticipate a point or see the structure of your argument. They are tools, no more. You will improve your writing only if you use them correctly and sparingly. You always have the option of using simple and familiar punctuation – full stops and commas.

Semi-colons can be used

1 **instead of full stops when you want to show a close link between two (usually short) sentences:**

```
Central banks always disagree with politicians about
inflation; that is their job.
```

```
Labour supply is represented by line S; as wages rise,
more workers join the labour market.
```

You can check your use of the semi-colon quite simply; if the two parts of the sentence are closely linked and could each form a sentence, you can choose to use a semi-colon. If in doubt, write two sentences and rephrase if necessary.

Look back at the extract 'Caring for the patient . . .' on p. 24. Try using a semi-colon instead of a full stop to link the first two sentences. Do you prefer this?

2 **to separate items in a list (instead of commas) when each item has several words:**

```
He would find out that many more men were enfranchised;
that political representation was improved; that political
parties had more definite identities and policies;  and
that religious emancipation was a fact.
```

Don't overdo this construction: the student who wrote this had six more items in the list of findings.

Colons

Colons are used to show that something linked is to follow, often a list or an explanation.

```
Sweden, however, offers a less harsh solution: active labour-
market policies.
```

```
Beyond these challenges lies a more fundamental one: customer
service.
```

6.4 Using bullet points

Bullet points are a useful alternative to semi-colons when you are setting out a list. Look at the two ways of presenting a long sentence listing several items shown in the examples below.

Example 1: Using a colon and semi-colons

> We assess students for a whole host of reasons. Here are some of the most commonly identified ones: motivation; creating learning activities; for feedback to the student, identifying strengths and weaknesses; for feedback to staff, on how well the message is getting across; to judge performance (grade/degree classification).

Example 2: Using bullet points

We assess students for a whole host of reasons. Here are some of the most commonly identified ones:

- motivation

- creating learning activities

- for feedback to the student, identifying strengths and weaknesses

- for feedback to staff, on how well the message is getting across

- to judge performance (grade/degree classification).

The text in these two extracts is identical. In Example 1, the the colon marks the end of the stem statement and introduces the list, which is set out using semi-colons to separate the items in the list. In Example 2, the new line for each item gives the eye (and the brain) sufficient guidance as to when one point ends and the next begins. Additional punctuation is unnecessary. The only capital letter needed is the first, and, of course, the sentence ends with a full stop.

There are numerous examples of the use of bullet points in this series. They are a useful way of setting out a list, especially when you want your reader to pause over each item. There is a knack to setting them out so the eye moves easily from one point to another.

A point to watch

Make sure your core statement connects equally well with each item in your list, whether you use bullets or write continuously. Look at this:

Students can use portfolios to demonstrate:

- the range of their achievements

- showing the quality of their products

- the tutors can see how well they have progressed in competence.

In this example, the stem statement works for the first item, but not for the second and third. The writer has stopped thinking.

Activity: Using bullet points

Rewrite the sentence above in three different ways.

1 Use the core statement above and rewrite the items to make them follow correctly.

2 Rewrite, using the following core statements in turn:

a Students can use portfolios:

b Portfolios have a number of uses:

Check your version with mine in the feedback section.

6.5   What next?

You need to think now about how to incorporate anything new you have learnt from this section in your day-to-day writing. Below are some suggestions.

1   Check, edit and rewrite your work

- Read your work critically before you hand it in, both for sense and for accuracy. This has been said many times before, but people are often really reluctant to check and edit their writing. Is it the sense of racing for the deadline? Phew! Or is a dread of the work involved? Whatever holds you back from reading and checking, deal with it . . . and check everything carefully. If you do not undertake this kind of check, you are placing unecessary barriers to communication in the way of your reader . . . with all the loss of goodwill that this entails.

- Do you see your own mistakes? Do you skim-read when you should proof-read? Are you too familiar with the work? Leave it, ideally for a day, although a few minutes' break may be enough to enable you to come back to it with a fresh eye.

- Read sticky sections out loud. If it sounds odd to you, your reader will be struggling too.

- Ask someone else to read it for you, and act on their comments.

2   Keep your eyes open

Pay close attention to the punctuation of your reading matter, whatever it is. This will help you to gain a sense of the styles used by different writers, from popular journalists to specialists in your subject. Take, say, one paragraph in each reading session, and see if you can explain the use of the punctuation in it.

3   Hear sense

Try using a tape recorder. You can experiment with this in a number of ways.

- Record yourself reading a short extract of something and play it back, stopping to give yourself time to write it down. Compare your punctuation with the original.

- Try this with your own work. Record what you would like to say, and worry about the punctuation afterwards when you write it down. This can be particularly useful with introductions, or if you find you have got stuck.

The message here is that you need to apply a new skill and practise it to be confident in its use.

Activity: What next?

Below is an extract from *The Economist* for you to work on while you are thinking about how to develop your own programme of punctuation awareness. It is reproduced without punctuation: this is for you to add. When you feel you have a viable version, compare it with the original, reproduced in the feedback section.

The break-up of Yugoslavia has been the first real test of how the democracies will cope with wars of conscience it has produced all the predictable symptoms first the official flinching away from the dangers of intervention next the public demand that something be done then the agonised attempt to to find a more or less cost-free way of doing something what has has been happening in ex-Yugoslavia will happen is already happening in other parts of the ex-communist world similar things have long been going on in Africa and parts of Asia the crises of conscience will multiply the more of them there are the likelier it is that a decision will eventually be made to go and rescue the poor devils and pay the price for doing the right thing otherwise the democracies could wake up one morning to realise that they have let the world break into two parts their own part will be an archipelago of comfortable civility outside the archipelago other people will be suffering awful things in Europe the awfulness could be going on not far from the gates of Rome Vienna Warsaw and Budapest the new world democrats will discover to their dismay has no order it is even more anarchically brutal than the old one.

(*The Economist*, 5 September 1992)

The writer of this extract is a professional journalist who uses a range of sentence structures and punctuation devices. You may have suggested perfectly correct alternatives, particularly where semi-colons and colons are used. Look at the differences between journalistic and academic writing – language, tone, sentence structure, punctuation, paragraphing. Enjoy the insight into how writers write, and the feeling of control that comes when you find you can put across exactly what you want to say to your reader by polishing and refining the way you say it.

6.2: Comma watch: Activity

Extract A

Comma	Use	Explanation
1	2A	Non-essential phrase at the beginning of a sentence.
2	2A	Another phrase at the beginning of a sentence.
3 and 4	2B	A pair, marking a phrase in the middle of a sentence.
5 and 6	1	Marking off items in a list.
7	2A	A clause at the beginning of a sentence.

Extract F

Comma	Use	Explanation
1	1	Between a series, or list, of verbs.
2 and 4	2	A pair, marking a phrase in the middle of a sentence.
3	1	Between a series, or list, of adjectives.

Extract G

Comma	Use	Explanation
1	2A	A phrase at the beginning of a sentence.

Extract D

Comma	Use	Explanation
1 and 2	2B	Non-essential phrase in the middle of a sentence.
3 and 4	2B	Non-essential phrase (although interesting) in the middle of a sentence.
5		Writer's choice. Used here to give a longer pause.
6, 7 and 8	2B	Used in pairs, to mark non-essential phrases.
9	2A	Marking a phrase at the beginning of the sentence.
10, 11, 12, 13	1	Items in a list.

6.4: Using bullet points: Activity

You may have come up with something along these lines:

```
1  Students can use portfolios to demonstrate:

      •    the range of their achievements

      •    the quality of their products

      •    progression from their original level of competence.
```

```
2a Students can use portfolios:
```

- to demonstrate the range of their achievements
- to show the quality of their products
- to provide evidence of their progress from their original level of competence.

```
b  Portfolios have a number of uses:
```

- to enable students to demonstrate the range of their achievements and the quality of their products
- to enable staff to assess students' progress from their original level of competence.

Alternatively, you may choose to use semi-colons and write continuously.

For example:

1 Students can use portfolios to demonstrate: the range of their achievements; the quality of their products; progression from their original level of competence.

6.5: What next? Activity

The break-up of Yugoslavia has been the first real test of how the democracies will cope with wars of conscience. It has produced all the predictable symptoms: first the official flinching away from the dangers of intervention; next the public demand that something be done; then the agonised attempt to to find a more or less cost-free way of doing something. What has has been happening in ex-Yugoslavia will happen – is already happening – in other parts of the ex-communist world. Similar things have long been going on in Africa and parts of Asia. The crises of conscience will multiply. The more of them there are, the likelier it is that a decision will eventually be made to go and rescue the poor devils, and pay the price for doing the right thing.

Otherwise the democracies could wake up one morning to realise that they have let the world break into two parts. Their own part will be an archipelago of comfortable civility. Outside the archipelago, other people will be suffering awful things. In Europe the awfulness could be going on not far from the gates of Rome, Vienna, Warsaw and Budapest. The new world, democrats will discover to their dismay, has no order; it is even more anarchically brutal than the old one.

(*The Economist*, 5 September 1992)

7 Writing paragraphs

The last chapter ended with two points concerning how to learn about writing: focus from time to time on the detail of how other people write; and try drawing on what you learn from this in your own writing. This chapter is based on these two approaches. A distinction is made here between activities that involve looking at writing (**In detail**, shown with a spectacles icon), and activities that involve you in some sort of writing (shown with the usual **Activity** icon). Feedback on the looking/checking activities (where any is necessary) is in the main text. Feedback on the writing activities is given at the end of the chapter.

7.1   The reader's perspective

'Need to pay attention to writing coherent paragraphs.'

'A 2-page paragraph?'

'Arrange information in coherent paragraphs.'

'Do not write one-sentence paragraphs.'

Comments such as these show that the reader – here, the tutor – is finding your work hard going. It is bad news for the writer. It means that your reader is having problems with

- seeing your main points

- following your argument

- seeing the structure of your written work

- seeing how the writing connects with the title.

In short, comments about paragraphs are really comments about structure and argument, which is why it is so important to know how to use the conventions of paragraph writing when you write.

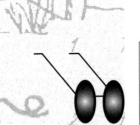

In detail

Put yourself in the place of the reader in a hurry.

- What is the main idea in each of the following paragraphs in the appendix?

    i) Extract A   ii) Extract B   iii) Extract C

- In which sentence is this idea most clearly stated?

I hope you agree that in each case the first sentence gives the clearest statement of what the paragraph is about. If this is what you expected, you will know how helpful it is to find yourself in a familiar landscape. Consciously or not, as a reader, you made use of the way paragraphs are put together. Your task as a writer is to offer the same service to your readers.

7.2 Paragraph structure

Paragraphs have a structure

- A paragraph has a main idea.

- This main idea is usually expressed clearly in one sentence, the 'topic sentence'.

- This topic sentence is usually the first in the paragraph.

- Paragraphs have a structure: a beginning, a middle and an end. The sentences in the middle explain, develop, illustrate or modify the main idea in the topic sentence. The last sentence often returns to the idea in the topic sentence to show how it has developed.

In detail

Turn to the extract on ex-Yugoslavia on p. 33. Do these paragraphs follow the pattern given above? For each, pick out

- the beginning: the topic sentence

- the middle: explanation, illustration, development

- the end: the link back to the topic sentence.

They do, don't they? Note especially how the last sentence works: it links back to the topic sentence, not to repeat it, but to show how the argument has moved on. It also looks ahead to the topic sentence of the next paragraph.

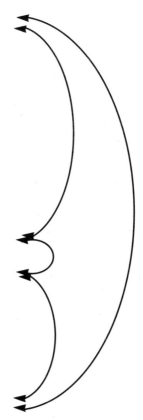

1	*Topic sentence*	The break-up of Yugoslavia has been the first real test of how the democracies will cope with wars of conscience. It has produced all the predictable
2	*Explanation*	symptoms: first the official flinching away from the dangers of intervention; next the public demand that
	and	something be done; then the agonised attempt to to find a more or less cost-free way of doing something.
	development	What has been happening in ex-Yugoslavia will happen – is already happening – in other parts of the ex-
3	*Illustration*	communist world. Similar things have long been going on in Africa and parts of Asia. The crises of conscience
4	*Comment*	will multiply. The more of them there are, the likelier it is that a decision will eventually be made to go and rescue
5	*Conclusion*	the poor devils, and pay the price for doing the right thing.
1	*Topic sentence*	Otherwise the democracies could wake up one morning to realise that they have let the world break into two
2	*Explanation*	parts. Their own part will be an archipelago of comfortable civility. Outside the archipelago, other
3	*Illustration*	people will be suffering awful things. In Europe the awfulness could be going on not far from the gates of
4	*Comment*	Rome, Vienna, Warsaw and Budapest. The new world, democrats will discover to their dismay, has no order;
5	*Conclusion*	it is even more anarchically brutal than the old one.

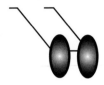

In detail

Turn to Extract D (in the appendix). Approach it in the following manner.

- Read the first sentence. Look up. Decide what you think the paragraph will be about.

- Read the rest. Were you right?

- Read the last sentence. Underline two words that mirror a key word in the first. Does this sentence repeat the first, or does it show a progression in thinking? What do you think the next paragraph will be about?

Each paragraph develops a main idea. This main idea in the topic sentence leads on from the paragraph before. The last sentence links with the topic sentence and points the way to the main idea in the next paragraph.

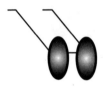

In detail

Skim-read the first three paragraphs in this guide. You know where to find the main idea. Look at the links between

- the last sentence of one paragraph and the first of the next

- the end of the third paragraph and the topic sentence of the first.

Paragraph structure has a purpose

It makes it easier

- **to read**; skim-reading is easier because the main idea is first. Close reading is easier because you have a general idea of what the text is about, and you know that one idea is developed before you move on to the next.

- **to plan**; each paragraph develops a single main point. You can link related points and plan the overall structure.

- **to write**; start with a clear statement of the point you are making, then add detail. Start a new paragraph when you start a new point.

7.3 How to write paragraphs

As a writer, you can approach writing paragraphs in a systematic way. Think of this as a paragraph plan.

A paragraph plan

1 **Start with the topic sentence**

- to express the main idea.

2 **Explain or define any abstract, key or problematic terms**

- to clarify the topic sentence.

3 **Show your evidence**

- to support your main idea or argument in the topic sentence.

4 **Comment on the evidence**

- to show how it supports or develops the main idea.

  If appropriate, mention other evidence (examples/studies/ experiments/interpretations) to widen the discussion.

5 **Conclude**

- to explain consequences or implications
- to show the development of the argument
- to link back to the idea in the topic sentence
- to link forward to the main idea in the next paragraph
- (in the first and last paragraphs of an essay or section) to show the link with the title or section heading.

Talking to your reader

The paragraph plan is a commonsense structure for writing. In conversational exchanges with people, you run through this process all the time: you say something, explain what you mean, tell the person why you think it, respond to their queries and comments – this is dialogue. When you write, you are doing something similar: you enter into a dialogue with your reader but, because your reader is invisible, your prose is continuous. Your reader comes to your writing in an inquiring frame of mind. Your task as a writer is to anticipate the reader's queries, and answer them almost before they have formulated them. The process goes something like this.

Reader: *So what's cooking?*

Writer: This is the point I want to make, the idea I
            want you to see.   **1 Topic sentence**

Reader: *Ah, I see. Tell me more.*

Writer: Let me explain . . .
                                                               2 Explain, define

Reader: *I see. What evidence do you base this on?*

Writer: Here's my evidence. These
            studies/experiments came up with pretty
            much the same findings, with slight
            variations . . .   **3 Show your evidence**

Reader: *I see. How does this connect with the point you
            are making?*

Writer: Like this. I think some of the points that
            come out of this study/experiment show
            that . . .   **4 Comment on the evidence**

Reader: *Fair enough. So where does this leave us?*

Writer: I've shown that the point I started with is
            a solid one and it makes you think
            that the next thing we should be thinking
            about is . . .   **5 Conclude**

Reader: *What is the next thing then? . . .*

. . . and you move on to the main point in the topic sentence of the next
            paragraph.

My thanks to Michael Hoey, Professor of Linguistics, University of Liverpool, for this helpful way of looking at the relationship between reader and writer.

Activity: Writing paragraphs

Below are two paragraphs from students' essays. For each decide

1   what is the main idea

2   what is the function of each sentence in the paragraph

3   whether the paragraph ends well

4   whether you think the paragraph is well written.

Number the sentences for ease of reference.

Paragraph 1

From the discussion section of a psychology practical report on the behaviour of people in discussion

Close personal acquaintance as a problem extends to the subject group, who all came from the same part of the room as the observers. As Hardy and Hayes (1987) observe, the sort of people who gravitate to the front of the room may be different from those who choose to sit at the back. Groups of people regularly in a lecture room tend to have a sense of 'place identity' (Proshansky, 1978, cited in Deaux and Wrightsman, 1988) and will be affected by each other and the relationships between them – the theory of propinquity (Festinger, Schachter and Back, 1950, cited in Deaux and Wrightsman, 1988). They were also volunteers and so may be of a more self-assertive nature. Certainly they were not representative of the population as a whole and might have been better selected randomly.

Paragraph 2

From an essay, 'Assess the relative importance of conscious public planning in shaping land use and urban form in the inner city since 1945'

In the early 1980s the Thatcher government made inner city regeneration a top priority. By encouraging a free enterprise spirit and easing planning constraints on new development in these areas, they believed the resulting investment and employment would end this economic decline. To this end they implemented two main policies: Enterprise Zones and Urban Development Corporations. Development under these policies is encouraged by financial incentives, the provision of transport infrastructure and the relaxation of planning controls. Probably the most famous example of development under these schemes is the regeneration of London's docklands. Massive transformations have occurred in this area, not least of which is the construction of Canary Wharf Tower, the tallest free-standing building in Europe.

Ending paragraphs

The lack of a concluding sentence in paragraphs is widespread – even in otherwise good writing. Sometimes it attracts comments from lecturers:

'How does this link with your argument?'

'How is this relevant?'

Much more often it does not. But it matters: remember the computing tutor's comment at the beginning of this guide. If you don't make these links, your points lose impact and you don't get the credit for the research and thinking you have done. It is a small writing skill with immense impact on your reader.

> The message is **LINK.**
>
> - **Link the last sentence to the topic sentence.**
>
> - **Link the topic sentence to the title or the section heading.**

For more work on paragraphs, with lots of examples and activities, see Student Guide 5: *Writing Essays*, Section 5.

7.4 Links in a paragraph

Linking or coherence in writing works at a number of levels. In the last section you looked at how ideas and arguments are developed in a paragraph; here the focus is on the micro-level of words and phrases that guide the reader through text. These 'markers' are useful to you as a reader: phrases such as 'The second factor . . .' will often send you scurrying back through the text for the first factor which somehow you had missed. As a writer, phrases such as this help you demarcate your points and structure your thoughts.

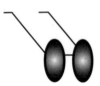

In detail

Take a look at how markers are used in this guide. Below are some examples.

- To show the order of points in an argument: *first, second, third,* in its simplest form.

    Find the equivalent words in the first paragraph of the piece on ex-Yugoslavia on p. 33 (The break-up. . .).

- To create an expectation of some kind of symmetry in how points are presented: *on the one hand . . . on the other.*

    Find a pair of phrases with this effect in the third paragraph on p. 1.

- To show a change of direction in argument: *but, however, yet, conversely.*

    Find two examples of this use in Extract A (appendix).

- To show that more arguments or evidence along the same lines is to follow: *moreover, also, of course, in addition.*

    Find two phrases which flag up important points to follow in Extract G.

- To show consequence*: so, thus, as a result.*

    Find an example in Extracts B and E.

- To show illustration: *for example, such as.*

    An illustration gives you the chance to check that you have understood, or made, the point itself.

- To show continuing discussion: *this, those, they.*

    Be careful when you use these. If there is any confusion about what they refer to, try substituting the word or phrase these markers stand for.

    (Student Guide 5: *Writing Essays*, Section 5.4, takes a close look at how an argument develops through links in the text.)

Activity: A closer look at structure

The sentences of the paragraph below are in a random order. Your task is to put them in order to form a coherent paragraph. Start with the sentence you think best expresses the idea of the whole. Use this as your topic sentence, and follow the paragraph plan as a framework for building the rest of the paragraph. Look at the detail of how sentences link together for clues to the order. Use a word processor if you can, so that you can cut and paste easily and try different sequences. When you have a paragraph you feel hangs together, compare it with the original in the feedback section.

The paragraph comes from the middle of a section of a long report. The section heading is

The private market for electric vehicles (EVs)

They are prepared to wait until the commercial and the public transport sectors have born the brunt of the development costs before private EVs become cost-effective to build.

At present there are several obstacles preventing the general public from purchasing EVs.

The European private vehicle market is without doubt the most difficult to exploit.

Prospective customers would have to live in or near a city where they work, have a high disposable income, operate two or more cars and have a strong commitment to caring for the environment.

The first is the cost.

There are other obstacles: in 3–4 years time, people will still choose a car for it's range and speed.

Even though most EVs are close to production or at an advanced prototype stage, nearly all manufacturers are unwilling to commit themselves to production runs as they know that prices are still too high for the private consumer.

This obviously has the effect of seriously reducing the market for EVs.

The EV is seen as suitable only for use as a small city runabout for shopping trips or short distance commuting.

This detailed work on how to write structured paragraphs should help you see the assumptions and expectations behind tutors' comments:

'A 2-page paragraph?'

Paragraphs have one main idea. If you carry on writing for two pages without a break, it tells your reader at a glance that you have not noticed when you moved on to a new idea. Typically, paragraphs are five to eight sentences long. Over two pages there are probably three or four major points that should be developed in separate paragraphs.

'Arrange information in coherent paragraphs.'

This is a comment about organization and planning. It looks as if this reader found points variously dotted about. At the planning stage, put together points that go together, pick out the main idea for each cluster of points, and write a paragraph for each.

'Do not write one-sentence paragraphs.'

A paragraph develops a single idea, as outlined in the paragraph plan. You cannot do this in one sentence. A string of single-sentence paragraphs tells your reader that you do not know how to develop your points or arguments – the shopping-list approach.

7.5   Getting it together

This chapter ends with an extended activity in developing single sentences into paragraphs. For this you need to draw on the work you have done so far, keeping the paragraph plan at the back of your mind. This is what you are working towards.

Read the extract below from a student's essay. The title is the same as for Paragraph 2 in Section 7.3 above.

Assess the relative importance of conscious public planning in shaping land use and urban form in the inner city since 1945.

As you read, think about how the writing could be improved.

> Urban employment   *Yes, but when did this start? What caused it?*
>
> In the last two decades the decline of manufacturing employment has led to a devastating effect on our lives.   *What evidence is there of its scale & effects?*
>
> On a regional scale there has been increasing dispersal of manufacturing away from the traditional core conurbation's to smaller free standing towns. There is also evidence that there has been change in the nature of manufacturing employment within urban areas.   *What evidence?*
>
> *Don't write one sentence paragraphs   Why?*   The 1947 planning system was of course aiming not at job loses but at encouraging the decentralisation of firms and jobs, from London in particular, to New Towns and Development areas.   *Did it work?*
>
> The inner city is no longer an attractive location for industry because of high land values and accessibility to these sites. New industry is likely to seek cheaper suburban or satellite town sites. Evidence suggests that firms simply ceased to operate as a result of redevelopment since their low profit margins made it impossible for them to move to purpose built high rent industrial premises.

In this short extract there are four main ideas, the basis for four paragraphs. As it stands, none of these four items functions as a paragraph: two are 'one-sentence paragraphs', and two are slightly longer. Nowhere does the writer develop the idea sufficiently to engage the reader in the subject, to give the reader an argument to follow, or to show the evidence for assertions made. The ideas are there, but they come across as a quick-fire set of bullets, not as a reasoned or developed argument.

Activity 1: From skeleton to paragraph

Your task is to act on the tutor's comments, and to rewrite the extract to develop the four ideas into full paragraphs of five to eight sentences. It does not matter if you do not know anything about the subject. A close reading will give you some pointers; then just make it up. When you have had a go, read the comments in the feedback section.

Activity 2: Using the paragraph plan

Recast the last paragraph in note form, following the paragraph plan in Section 7.3. Make whatever changes you think are necessary. Use points from the outline in the feedback section and invent any additional details you need.

Paragraph plan
1   The topic sentence
2   Explain or define
3   Show your evidence
4   Comment on the evidence
5   Conclude

As you worked on this small extract you may have found yourself wondering if it is all worth the effort. Is this not simply poor writing by a weak student which no amount of effort will turn into a good essay? I hope you dismissed such thoughts: this student had a good grasp of the subject, as the four main ideas show. The problem is that it is not evident in the written product.

Think back to the computing lecturer's comments on the first page. No, you do not get marked on your writing. Yes, of course it matters; there is this magical connection between good writing and high grades. I hope you can now see why: by observing the conventions of academic writing, specifically paragraph writing, you making effective use of the units of argument. A paragraph structure is a template for developing your ideas. Your readers share this template. Consciously or unconsciously, they are looking for this pattern when they read. Your job as a writer is to present your material in this form, not only to make it easier for your reader to read, but for you as a writer to achieve your purpose in writing – to be given the credit for communicating what you know and understand.

7.3: Writing paragraphs: Activity

My comments are given as numbered points corresponding to the specific questions in the activity.

Paragraph 1

1   The main idea is the problem the psychology researcher faces when the subjects of the study know the observers. This is clearly stated in the topic sentence.

2   Sentences 2 and 3 develop this. The student relates the problems she experienced with her study to those described in other studies. In sentence 4 she adds her own reflections.

3   The last sentence relates this discussion of problems back to the topic sentence, and moves on. It might have been better to select subjects at random.

4   This is a well structured paragraph, and easy to follow. It would be more readable if the long sentence (3) was rewritten as two separate sentences – one for each of the points that emerges from the two studies cited.

Paragraph 2

1   The main idea is the government's inner-city regeneration initiatives in the early 1980s. This is clearly stated in the topic sentence.

2   Sentence 2 expands and clarifies; 3 introduces the measures suggested in the topic sentence; 4 explains the working of these; 5 and 6 discuss a specific example.

3   There is no concluding sentence. Try adding one – something that links the Docklands development to the main point in the topic sentence.

4   With the addition of a concluding sentence, this is now a well written and well structured piece.

7.4: A closer look at structure: Activity

In this activity, you were asked to reconstruct a paragraph using clues in the text. You probably found it was a much harder exercise than you thought! Below is the original (slightly amended).

```
The European private vehicle market is without doubt the most
difficult to exploit. At present there are several obstacles
preventing the general public from purchasing EVs. The first
is the cost. Even though most EVs are close to production or
at an advanced prototype stage, nearly all manufacturers are
unwilling to commit themselves to production runs as they
know that prices are still too high for the private consumer.
They are prepared to wait until the commercial and the public
transport sectors have borne the brunt of the development
costs before private EVs become cost-effective to build. There
are other obstacles: in 3-4 years time, people will still
choose a car for its range and speed. The EV is seen as
suitable only for use as a small city runabout for shopping
trips or short distance commuting. Prospective customers would
have to live in or near a city where they work, have a high
disposable income, operate two or more cars and have a strong
commitment to caring for the environment. This obviously has
the effect of seriously reducing the market for EVs.
```

If you identified the topic sentence and the concluding sentence, you have the bones of the paragraph; you may have minor differences in the order in the middle. Two errors escaped this student's spellcheck. Did you spot them? (born/borne; it's/its) You could streamline some expressions: 'nearly all manufacturers are unwilling' 'few manufacturers are willing'. Any others?

7.5: From skeleton to paragraph: Activity

Ideally you should have four substantial paragraphs that develop the main idea in each of the topic sentences. In my version below, I have given pointers as to the content the reader wants to see.

Urban employment

In the last two decades the decline of manufacturing employment has had a devastating effect on our lives. *[A good topic sentence – but it needs a paragraph to develop the points suggested in the topic sentence: does 'manufacturing' need to be defined? What caused the decline? What are these 'devastating effects'? On what scale? Illustration and evidence are needed. 'Our lives' – whose lives? Are some people affected more than others? Responses to these questions would make a well developed paragraph of a sensible length – six to eight sentences.]*

On a regional scale there has been increasing dispersal of manufacturing away from the traditional core conurbations to smaller free standing towns. *[Another good topic sentence – but tell us more. Where are these located? What sort of manufacturing has moved in this way? An example or two?]* There is also evidence that there has been change in the nature of manufacturing employment within urban areas. *[This is also a substantial statement: it could be a topic sentence of a new paragraph, but here it marks a shift within the paragraph. Either way, give us some supporting detail: what is the nature of the change? What evidence is there for this statement? The concluding sentence should link these parallel developments, and point to the link with the topic sentence of the next paragraph.]*

The 1947 planning system was not aiming at job losses but at encouraging the decentralisation of firms and jobs, from London in particular, to New Towns and Development areas. *[Another good topic sentence in search of a paragraph. But as a reader I am puzzled by the sudden shift in time back to 1947. What is the connection with what has gone before? Should the section have started with this point? The missing paragraph needs to answer some questions: what was the thinking behind decentralisation? Did it work? The concluding sentence could pull back to the impact on the cities – and link with the next paragaph.]*

The inner city is no longer an attractive location for industry because of high land values and accessibility to these sites. *[This sounds like rather a sweeping statement. The wording should be more cautious and points substantiated with evidence. There are two substantial points in the topic sentence: high land values and accessibility. The points are just about there, but the reader has to dig for them – the writer has not made the links. Add a sentence about why land values are high, and what the problems of accessibility are.]* New industry is likely to seek cheaper suburban or satellite town sites. *[Presumably because land values are lower and accessibility easier. If so, say so.]* Evidence suggests that firms simply ceased to operate as a result of redevelopment since their low profit margins made it impossible for them to move to purpose-built high rent industrial premises. *[First mention of redevelopment. This looks like the explanation missing after the topic sentence. What evidence? Give it – and we have an illustration.]*

7.5 (2): Using the paragraph plan: Activity

Paragraph plan

1 **The topic sentence**

For many industries, the inner city is no longer an attractive location.

2 **Explain or define**

High land values – sites redeveloped (by speculative property developers? other players?) – high rents – old firms on low profit margins – unable to pay – out of business. Plus problems of access – traffic congestion – restrictions on lorries.

3 **Show your evidence**

London? Docklands?

4 **Comment on the evidence**

Relate this to high land values and accessibility.

5 **Conclude – to show consequences, relevance of example, and development of main idea in topic sentence.**

Industry moves to suburban or satellite towns – lower cost – better access. Consequences for inner cities.

Good spelling

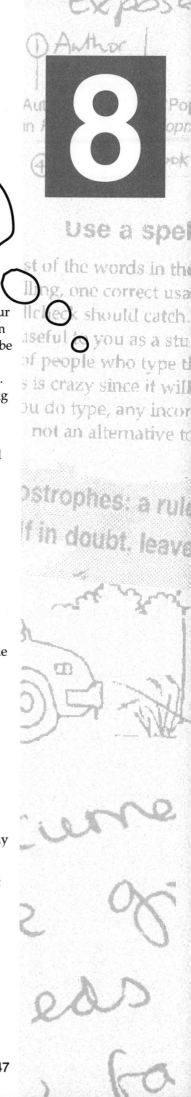

> 'I suggest you learn to use a spellcheck.'
> 'You must do something about your spelling.'
> 'Spelling.'
> 'Sp.'

You will not often get thoughtful and analytical comments about your spelling from your tutors in higher education. You may get a correction; you may have a word ringed; often you will have no indication at all that your tutor has noticed a wrong spelling. You can be pretty sure, however, that tutors and examiners do notice spelling mistakes, and, consciously or unconsciously, downwardly revise their opinion of your work as a result. If this happens, you are failing to achieve your objectives as a writer. This is why spelling matters.

Spelling is primarily a matter of impression management. Mistakes in spelling have a unique capacity to irritate your reader, especially when that reader is a lecturer, external examiner or potential employer. Spelling mistakes undoubtedly do place distractions in the path of your reader, but the annoyance they cause – and the damage to you as a writer – can seem out of proportion to the offence. Consider for a moment why this should be.

What messages do spelling mistakes give your reader? That

- you have not checked your work?

- you have been hasty and unstructured in your writing?

- you are being discourteous to your reader?

- a brick or two in the foundations of your education is missing? This is worrying to the tutor whose brief is to build the upper storey. In the future, you will have other readers to think about: potential employers can use any aspect of presentation as grounds for eliminating candidates, and spelling is an old favourite.

These are partial and slightly speculative explanations, but like it or not, spelling cannot be divorced from the content of your writing; it is a convention that forms part of the landscape that either welcomes or alienates your reader.

You, of course, may see it differently. Perhaps

- your spelling was 'good enough' before – for what was required of you then

- you are secretly unconvinced that spelling matters; in different circumstances this may have been so

- you have put an immense amount of effort into spelling in the past, and your current error rate represents a great improvement

- you accept that you are a 'bad speller'.

Whatever your history with spelling, and your tutor's particular bugbears, if you make frequent or specific spelling mistakes you need to work to correct them. This section offers nine pieces of advice on how to improve your spelling. See which you find useful.

8.1 Compile a personal hit list

What mistakes do you make? Go through a few pieces of work and pick out all your spelling mistakes. Since not all will have been highlighted by your tutor, ask a friend to check through with you.

—

8.2 Look for patterns of errors

See if you can group your errors into clusters of related spellings. You may find that you only have to work on one structure to resolve your spelling problem.

Look at this extract:

> Paul Unsheild reveals this plurality of conceptualization is related to systeme which are mutualy incompahble and assouated with the presence in souety of groupc which have different idedogies. He shews this histerically (1986) Conceptions differ between age groups, and differ greatly trans culturaly or ethnicaly. (Cunver and Stacey 1986) The differences between lay and professional perspectives on health are most pertinantly revealed by Ann Oakley (1986) in her study of

This is a fluent piece of writing. You feel that the writer is comfortable and in control of the complex process of drawing together references to different sources, but minor spelling mistakes place irritants in the path of the reader. A closer look shows that four of the five spelling mistakes in this short extract follow the same pattern – not doubling the 'l' in forming the adverb: mutual/mutually, historical/historically, etc. This is a simple spelling rule: learn it and you need never make this mistake again. It is also good tactics. If you make the same mistake ten times, you chalk up ten errors. Target your most frequent mistakes first for dramatic results.

8.3 Identify spelling patterns

There is more logic in English spelling than many people think. A few patterns can be seen at work in a lot of words: it helps to be aware of them. The patterns here are examples only.

1 The silent 'e'

At school, you may have come across the 'magic e' – the silent 'e' that makes the vowel say its name. This is as good a way as any of remembering the effect the silent 'e' has on a simple syllable: the short vowel becomes a long vowel. The short a in 'mad' becomes the long 'a' in 'made'. Consider the effect of adding a silent 'e' to the following:

wag, pet, win, hop, cut.

short words such are unlikely to cause you problems, but the pattern can be helpful where these syllables are part of a longer word.

Activity

Underline the part of each word below where this pattern applies.

deactivate	replacement	completely	extreme
organize	empire	envelope	removed
biomolecule	produced		

Note the pattern you are studying – the silent 'e' here – in a short section of anything you are reading. Underline examples in the extract on ex-Yugoslavia (p. 33).

---

2 Double or single consonant?

This is another pattern with frequent application. Again, it helps if you can identify short and long vowels; you can work out the likely spelling from the sound of the word.

Consider **shine, shining, shinning**. This last might describe a cat burglar's ascent of a wall. The other two have more to do with light.

The pattern is that, when the vowel is short, the consonant is doubled. When the vowel is long, there is only one consonant. For example:

mat	**matting**
mate	**mating**
bit	**bitter**
bite	**biting**

Activity

Mark the long vowels in the examples above with a bar (–) above the letter (as in a dictionary). Mark the short vowels with a little saucer (ᶜ).

Observe this pattern at work in your reading.

8.4 Take a technical interest in words

- Be aware of syllables:

    cor-res-pon-dence

    de-fin-ite-ly

- Be aware of sections of words:

    pre (in front of); **fix** (attached to); **es** (plural)

    dis (prefix); **sat-is** (Latin = enough); **fac** (Latin = makes); **tion** (suffix, noun form)

- Be aware of related words:

correspondence – respond – response

definitely – define – finite – definition

- Nudge yourself into becoming interested in the history of words: when the word came into the language, from which culture, how its meaning has evolved.

Activity

In your idle moments, look up a few words in a good dictionary, such as the *Shorter Oxford Dictionary*. You could start with a couple of the following: electric, window, wheel, star, school, cotton, dandelion, town, justice, private, hypothesis, homosexual, budget, boycott, myth, ammonia, crucial, commuter, disincentive.

Here are two:

town: from the Northern European languages including Celtic and Old Irish. The 'tun', 'ton', 'dun' is to be found in modern place names – London, Tonbridge. Note the changes in meaning: from *fort*, to *enclosure, manor, land of a village*, group of *buildings*, to the modern *'town'*.

homosexual: 'homo' comes from the Greek meaning 'same', not Latin for 'man'. Sex is from the Latin.

(Williams, 1989, p. 215)

8.5   Target particular confusions

To use these correctly, you need to know

- the meaning
- the usage.

Some commonly confused words are

their	**they're**	**there**
effect	**affect**	
incident	**incidence**	
complement	**compliment**	
practice	**practise**	
dependant	**dependent**	
discrete	**discreet**	
weather	**whether**	
council	**counsel**	
procede	**proceed**	

8.6   Find out more about learning theory

How do we learn to spell? How do you learn? Current learning theory identifies a number of approaches. These include

- the **visual** approach – learning the look and shape of a word
- the **auditory** approach – learning the component sounds of a word
- the **logical** or **syntactic** approach – learning through grammar and word study.

To these you may add **individual methods** that work for you

- jingles
- mnemonics
- a mental picture.

8.7 Look for help

If your problems with spelling go beyond the sorts of approaches suggested here you may have a specific difficulty, and need to refer yourself to a specialist within your institution. This is a positive step, not a negative one: you may gain access to specialist tuition, advice on helpful resources, concessions, such as permission to use a word processor (and spellcheck), extra time in exams. A referral and assessment will, in any case, establish whether you have a major or a minor difficulty, and set you on your way to sorting it out. It is far better to take this positive move than to puzzle over a string of inexplicably low grades.

8.8 The hit list

All the spellings below have either been taken directly from students' work, or compiled from tutors' lists of particular bugbears. By whatever means you choose, make sure you spell these words correctly.

Activity

Go through the list at speed, marking those that sound like another word, and could therefore slip through a spellcheck.

Mark any you hesitate over, or tend to misspell.

rein	tendency	different	experience
implement	definitely	losing	their
correspondence	grammar	decision	pursue
formerly	stationary	council	supersede
manner	habit	laid	integrate
principal	responsibility	fulfilment	occasionally
occasion	led	undoubtedly	separate
profession	excite	original	finance
practise	independent	accommodation	affect
existing	unsuccessful	effect	discussion
exercise	strengthening	practice	incorporated
inevitably	inherently	increasingly	herd
acknowledgement	interrelated	there	competence
commitment	primarily	quantities	manor
implementation	components	democratically	lead
occurred	knowledgeable	environment	guarantee
harass	perceive		

Devise ways of helping yourself to learn any that are problematic for you.

8.9 Use a spellcheck

Most of the words in the hit list above should never be misspelt – there is one correct spelling, one correct usage and no confusion over meaning. These are the words a spellcheck should catch. If you have not already learnt keyboard skills, do so now. It will be useful to you as a student and when you move into employment. Funnily enough, a lot of people who type their work still do not remember or bother to use a spellcheck. This is crazy since it will pcik up mis-types as well as actual speling mistakes. Of course, if you do type, any incorrect usage will show all the more clearly. A spellcheck is a useful tool, not an alternative to reading your work critically.

The passage below gives a taste of the points a spellcheck does not pick up.

> The prefect automated tool for analyzing spelling hasn't yet been invested. In most peoples' judgement, even the least skilful personnel assistance has earned her keep when he has caught a dozen typos that the computer failed too recognise. Many a principle lecturer, who has spelled the name of his subject aria wrong and mistook the faculty to witch his school belongs, has benefited from the focused eye of the personnel assistance, but would have been exposed as a charlady had the job bin left to a computer.
>
> In some ways the machine is hypercritical, in others, such as those that are dependent on distinctions between english and american spilling, it's response is definitively sub-standard. Pre-eminently the marvellous machine seems positively encyclopaedic in its tolerance for various spellings, and its mane offense is to be unable to realise that a coordinated attitude to stile is needed. Is it so oblivious to the rudiments of consistence that it can allow an English person to both "practice" and 'practise' in a single sentence, yet so prejudiced that it will not permit a Scotch to writer in his / her own language unless s/he confirms to some notional standard determined by a soft-where buff.
>
> As for grammar and syntax . . . English, as she is writ by them as nose, is nun of the computers concern. And confusable words – i.e. words that in an other contact would be ripe but in this one are wrong – are quiet beneath its apprehension. It couldn't even spot (so to speak) Doctor Spooner's shoving leopard!
>
> (From Rosemary Roberts, *'Writing for the Publishing Field'*, a booklet for students taking publishing courses, Oxford Brookes University)

Activity

Pick out categories of errors the spellcheck let through, and find examples of each from the passage.

Using sources in academic work

> *'Reference?'*
>
> *'This is not a reference – you do not refer to it.'*
>
> *'Where did you get this from?'*
>
> *'Yes, but you need to take into account Jones and Woodhouse on this too.'*
>
> *'EVIDENCE??'*

Comments such as these suggest two things:

- that you need to get to grips with referencing fully and accurately

- that you are not confident about how to draw on other writers and thinkers in your academic writing.

The first point is a simple one to remedy. You need to find out what form of referencing your department prefers, try it out and use it. If this is what you need, turn to Section 9.4 below. Most university libraries also have useful leaflets with more detailed advice.

The second point is trickier. It is less to do with the mechanics of referencing than with your confidence in using the conventions of the academic environment in which you find yourself. Below are some of the problems people experience.

9.1 Some common problems

Problems with academic style?

There may be a mismatch between what you think you should be doing and what is expected of you. British academic style is to look at a subject from several angles, to debate and discuss different interpretations of the 'facts', events or theories. If you see your task as presenting facts, it may lead you to presenting material uncritically – without acknowledging where you got it from. This may lead to comments such as

> *'Is this so?? Who said?'*
>
> *'Sure, but how have different commentators responded?'*

Problems with confidence?

Where you feel a writer has expressed something really well, it is tempting to copy out a chunk. This may lead to comments such as

> *'Whose comment is this? Yours? or Jones and Woodward?'*

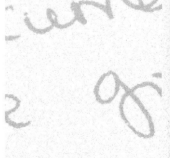

Problems with expression?

You may hesitate about when you need to quote a writer word for word, and when you need only refer to their findings and comment on them. This can lead to awkward expression and confusion for the reader over who said what:

'Too much quotation.'

'You don't need all this detail about the study – get on to your point.'

Section 9.4 offers some pointers to dealing with these problems. You will find guidance on building an argument, using evidence and drawing on other people's ideas in Student Guide 5: *Writing Essays*, sections 5.4 to 5.6.

9.2 Making tracks

What is it you are doing when you set out on an inquiry? Think of it as a day out in the country.

You set off down the motorway . . .

turn off on an A road . . .

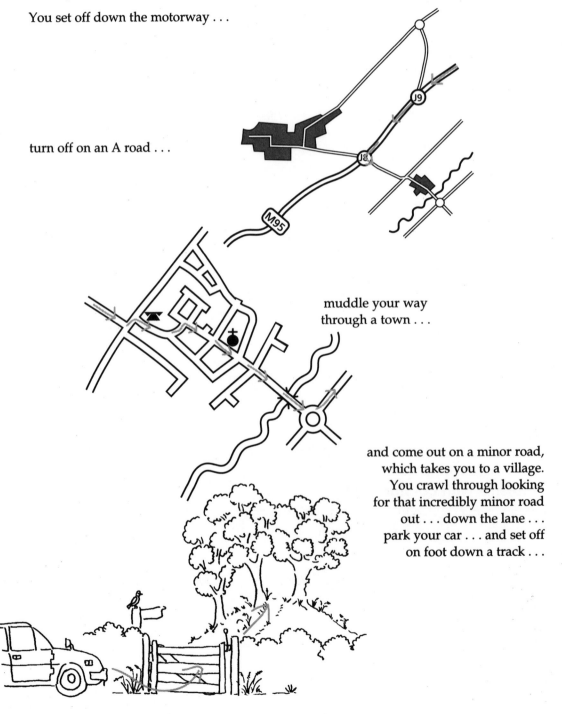

muddle your way
through a town . . .

and come out on a minor road,
which takes you to a village.
You crawl through looking
for that incredibly minor road
out . . . down the lane . . .
park your car . . . and set off
on foot down a track . . .

You turn off the track onto a footpath, into the woods. You feel as if no one has ever been there before, because you're on your own . . . but they have, of course, because paths are made by feet that went that way before. But in a sense you are on your own. There is no one to tell you what to see, and no reason for thinking that anyone has seen exactly what you now see.

This is a reasonably good description of the academic process.

- If you never leave the motorway, you never see anything. So go beyond the minimum reading of course notes, handouts, basic text.

- If you stick to the footpaths all day, you'll never get anywhere. So start with the core knowledge you need, and from there move into detail as you refine your process of inquiry. In this way, you link the specific with the broader themes of your subject.

- And, crucially, leave tracks, footprints, records, to show where you have been. This is so that other people can follow your route, choose where to diverge, and set out on their own paths. This is to do with record keeping and referencing.

9.3 A glimpse at the academic process

So how does it work in practice? This section is designed to show you why full and accurate record keeping is essential to the academic process. The records you keep at the research stage will form the basis of your bibliography when you have finished your piece of work.

Was Malthus right about population?

You've never heard of Malthus, let alone his theories on population, and you have to write an essay on this title. Where do you start?

Step 1: Fact finding

Ask questions:

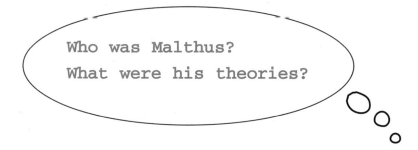

> Who was Malthus?
> What were his theories?

You set off to the library. Finding books on Malthus is not a problem. You pick one that looks a little more cheerful than the rest:

Malthus, by William Petersen.

Check the date of publication (1979 – a bit old, but OK for basic information) and survey it. Look for the answers to your two questions:

> Thomas Robert Malthus was born in 1766 and died in 1834. That he lived during a period of momentous and often tumultuous change is hardly a novel observation . . .

(See Student Guide 5: *Writing Essays*, Section 4.3, and Williams (1989) for a strategic approach to reading.)

You move on to his theories, and find a long extract quoted by Petersen:

> Difficult as it might be to double the average produce of [Britain] in twenty-five years, let us suppose if effected . . . During the next period of doubling, where will the food be found to satisfy the importunate demands of the increasing numbers? . . .
>
> It is a perfectly just observation of Mr Godwin that "there is a principle in human society by which population is perpetually kept down to the level of the means of subsistence." The sole question is, what is this principle?

This is followed by an explanation by the author of your book:

> Malthus began with two postulates: that "food is necessary to the existence of man" and that "the passion between the sexes is necessary and will remain nearly in its present state." If one grants the validity of these "fixed laws of nature", then it follows that the "power" of population to increase is "indefinitely greater" than the "power" of the earth to provide food. "Population, when unchecked, increases in a geometrical ratio. Subsistence increases only in an arithmetical ratio . . ."

And there you have it. Make notes, and be careful to distinguish who said what. Your notes will include:

- your words, as you record key points from Petersen's account
- Petersen's words, if you find something that he expresses so well/wittily/succinctly that you would lose the flavour if you tried to make notes in your own words
- Malthus's words quoted by Petersen (see above)
- Godwin's words, quoted by Malthus (see above).

You must also record the details of Petersen's book in a way that will enable

- you to trace it again easily if you need to
- your reader to follow up your researches if they want to
- your assessor to see your footprints in the research process. The bottom line of this is: where has this student been? What is the extent of their reading? What use have they made of other writers and commentators?

The book details you need to record are:

1 **Author(s), surname and initial(s):** *Petersen, W.*

2 **Year of publication:** *1979*

3 **(If applicable) Title of chapter or article:**

4 **Title of book or periodical:** *Malthus*

5 **(For books) Edition (if not first):**

   (For periodicals) (as appropriate): Volume / issue / month / page numbers

6 **Place of publication:** *London*

7 **Publisher:** *Heinemann*

If you record the details in this order, you have them ready for your full reference in the bibliography (see Section 9.5).

Little, if any, academic work will stop at the stage of basic factual information. Once you have established your baseline, you have to go beyond to the field of interpretation and conflict – both of views, and of the facts themselves.

Step 2: Interpretation and evidence

More questions:

> Was Malthus right?
>
> Was he right at the time? Did other commentators at the time think he was right or wrong?
>
> What have later commentators thought?
>
> How valid are these commentators?
>
> What use have they made of the available evidence on population figures?
>
> What are the facts about current population changes and about projected population changes?

Your task is now in sharper focus: in the light of the evidence available to you, do you think he was right or not? Your researches could take you to all corners of the library.

Another book

You would probably come by other books via a subject search. The following title comes at the topic from a different angle:

Patterns of Development: Resources, Policy and Economic Growth, by Richard M. Auty.

Date of publication 1995, good and recent. There is a useful index and a chapter with a section 'Population pressures'. . .

It is clear that the demographic transition model takes insufficient account of the important mediating role played by cultural factors. Societies where the status of women is not inferior are quickest to seize the opportunity to reduce family size (as in Communist China and Hindu India, for example, in contrast to Catholic Brazil and Muslim Egypt). Moreover, some researchers like Ward and Dubos (1972) argue that the potential of the green revolution in agriculture to raise living standards in the rural areas of Asia means that high urbanization may no longer be a prerequisite for completion of the demographic transition to population stability.

This suggests that a deceleration in population growth is not likely to occur humanely in an economically neglected and male-dominated rural society, such as that of much of sub-Saharan Africa . . .

Book details

1 Author(s), surname and initial(s): *Anty, R. M.*

2 Year of publication: *1995*

3 (If applicable) Title of chapter or article: *Population, technology and land: a soft-tech greening of Africa*

4 Title of book or periodical: *Patterns of Development*

5 (For books) Edition (if not first):

   (For periodicals) (as appropriate): Volume / issue / month / page numbers

6 Place of publication: *London*

7 Publisher: *Edward Arnold*

See Section 9.5 for the bibliographical reference.

Periodicals

The journal *Population Studies* contains an article 'Below Replacement Fertility in China? A Close Look at Recent Evidence'.

Read the beginning and end of the abstract.

China's State Family Planning Commission conducted a national survey in late 1992 following earlier surveys in 1988 and 1982. In April 1992 the Commission released statistics derived from the survey which implied that China's fertility had fallen below replacement level during the 1990s. How reliable are the statistics on which this extraordinary report was based? . . .

. . . our analysis suggests that the 1992 survey may have underreported births during these years by between 10 and 20 per cent. Even allowing for such underreporting, however, it seems likely that Chinese fertility did in fact fall to replacement level during the early 1990s.

Details of article

1 **Author(s), surname and initial(s):** *Feeney, G. and Jianhua, Y.*

2 **Year of publication:** *1994*

3 **(If applicable) Title of chapter or article:** *Below Replacement Fertility in China? A Close Look at Recent Evidence*

4 **Title of book or periodical:** *Population Studies*

5 **(For books) Edition (if not first):**

   (For periodicals) (as appropriate): *Volume: 48 / Issue: 3 / month: November / page numbers: 381-94*

6 **Place of publication:** *not given in a journal reference*

7 **Publisher:** *not given in a journal reference*

Your search may take you to newspapers, to the statistics collection, to databases, to a CD-ROM . . . but there will be a point at which you are ready to plan and write the essay. For help with this, see Student Guide 5: *Writing Essays*. If you have noted the full details of the sources you have consulted, your bibliography will be easy to compile without the irritating and time-consuming process of retracing your steps.

It is worth giving some thought to how you organize your notes and references. In the early stages of a library trawl you might like to try the following suggestions.

- note the full details of materials (books, articles) that look as if they might be useful when you first find them, whether or not you later track down or use the material. You can then look for the actual piece at any time without returning to the reference source.

- try using cards for references and notes. Put each reference on one side of the card, and brief notes to remind you of the content, key points and how it might be useful on the other. This makes it easier to group sources, ideas and themes, and to resort as you change your ideas. It helps to keep your notes tidy, and it also saves time, because you haven't got the space to make copious notes on something that turns out to be irrelevant!

9.4 Using sources in your writing

You then have to work out how you will make use of your evidence in the argument of your essay. There is no scope for factual presentation; this material is the evidence you will use to support your points. If you think back to the paragraph plan (Section 7.3), your references to your evidence will come in the middle of a paragraph, since you will be using this evidence to illustrate a point or support an argument. You will decide on how to make the link between your point and your evidence: whether to report, reference or quote.

Reporting

When you report, you paraphrase. This means you pick out the points you want to discuss and express them in your own words, before going on to comment on them and discuss them. When you do this, you must make it clear whose ideas you are discussing and where you got them from. Look at the example in the extract from Auty above:

Moreover, some researchers like Ward and Dubos (1972) argue that . . .

You might find yourself writing something like the following.

```
Petersen (1979) points out that Malthus lived in an age of rapid
social change . . .

Auty (1995) identifies the position of women as key to the
reduction of family size. A consequence of this, he suggests, is
that, in male-dominated societies, rapid population growth is
likely to continue . . .

A recent study  of fertility in China by Feeney and Jianhua
(1994) seems to confirm the evidence of earlier studies
indicating that fertility fell to replacement level in the early
1990s.
```

You can introduce other people's work with phrases like

As X points out . . .

Research by Y (1993) indicates that . . .

X and Y (1994) found that . . .

If you want to distance yourself from the views expressed in the work to which you are referring, or to present work in such a way that leaves it open to you to discuss alternative interpretations, you can do so by using more tentative language:

X argues that . . .

Y's study (1991) had similar findings . . .

In her study of . . ., Y (1986) claims that . . .

This method of making brief references to a source in your text is the Harvard system, probably now the most used in British universities. It is an economical way of referring to a source without interrupting the flow of the text. You then list the full details of the source in the bibliography (see Section 9.5 below).

Referencing

This is similar to reporting, but you discuss the work directly, and include the reference to the author with the date of the publication in brackets.

```
Malthus lived in an age of rapid social change
(Petersen, 1979) . . .

The position of women is key to the reduction of family size
(Auty,1995). A consequence of this is that, in male-dominated
societies, rapid population growth is likely to continue . . .

A recent study of fertility in China seems to confirm the
evidence of earlier studies which indicate that fertility fell
to replacement level in the early 1990s (Feeney and Jianhua,
1994).
```

The effect of this style is to make your writing more vigorous and less tentative. The views of the author you are drawing on appear to be closer to your own. (The extract from a student's essay (Paragraph 1, Section 7.3, above) provides useful examples on how to refer in this way.)

Quoting

You want to quote only when it is especially important for your reader to see and appreciate the precise wording of the original. You may choose to do this to

- provide your reader with the original when you are discussing the text in detail

- illustrate a point precisely

- discuss interpretations of a well-known authority

- respect the wording of the original, when the impact would be lost if you tried to explain or paraphrase it.

Quotation marks are used so your reader can distinguish the words of the other writer from yours at a glance. Use the exact wording, punctuation and spelling of the original:

```
Malthus' theory on population growth was that 'Population, when
unchecked, increases in geometrical ratio. Subsistence increases
only in an arithmetical ratio .  . .' The key phrase here
is '. . .
```

It is helpful to your reader to give the precise page reference to an extract you quote. If you want to quote an extract that already contains a quotation, show this by using double quotation marks (if you normally use single) for the extract the author is quoting:

```
Malthus described as 'perfectly just' Godwin's observation that
"there is a principle in human society by which population is
perpetually kept down to the level of the means of subsistence."
The question Malthus then poses is as valid today as it was when
he wrote: 'The sole question is, what is this principle?'
(Malthus, quoted by Petersen, 1979, p. 46).
```

Quotations

For a **short quotation**

- run it into your text

- use quotation marks, single or double, as long as you are consistent.

For a **long quotation**

- do not use quotation marks

- indent the passage

- distinguish the presentation from the rest of your text – for example, by leaving a line between your text and the extract and reducing the size of the quoted block.

(For an example, see the extract from Malthus's writings quoted by Petersen above.)

However you decide to refer to other people's writing, the important thing for your reader is to see what sense you have made of it. Always comment on sources you make use of. This is how you join in the academic process and debate.

9.5   Writing your bibliography

If you have the full details of the sources you have consulted, this is straightforward.

The Harvard system

In the Harvard (or author–date) system the bibliography at the end of your text is arranged alphabetically, with the elements of the reference in the same order as the book details outlined in Section 9.3. The bibliography for the sources drawn on in this chapter would be as follows:

A book reference

② Year of publication

① Author   ③ Title of chapter

Auty, R. M. (1995). 'Population, technology and land: a soft-tech greening of Africa', in *Patterns of Development.* London, Edward Arnold.

④ Title of book   ⑦ Publisher

⑥ Place of publication   [⑤ Edition N/A]

Another book reference

①   ②

Petersen, W. (1979). *Malthus.* London, Heinemann.   [③ N/A]

④   ⑥   ⑦

A journal reference

② Year of publication

① Authors   ③ Title of article

Feeney, G. and Jianhua, Y. (1994). 'Below replacement fertility in China? A close look at recent evidence', *Population Studies*, Vol. 48, No. 3, pp. 381–94.

④ Title of journal   ⑤ Details (Vol, No, pages)

[⑥ N/A]

[⑦ N/A]

The British Standard system

This system of referencing uses the same elements, but arranges them in a different order, with the date at the end. The real difference to you as a writer is not so much the organization of the bibliography, but the method of referring to the source in your text.

In the text

In the British Standard system, you number your references (ideally in superscript) in the text. This refers your reader to the items in your bibliography in the order in which you refer to them in the text. The examples above would become:

> Petersen[1] points out that Malthus lived in an age of rapid social change . . .

> The position of women is key to the reduction of family size[2] A consequence of this is that, in male-dominated societies, rapid population growth is likely to continue . . .

> A recent study of fertility in China[3] seems to confirm the evidence of earlier studies indicating that fertility fell to replacement level in the early 1990s.

In the bibliography

The bibliography for these sources in the British Standard system would be presented as follows.

A book reference

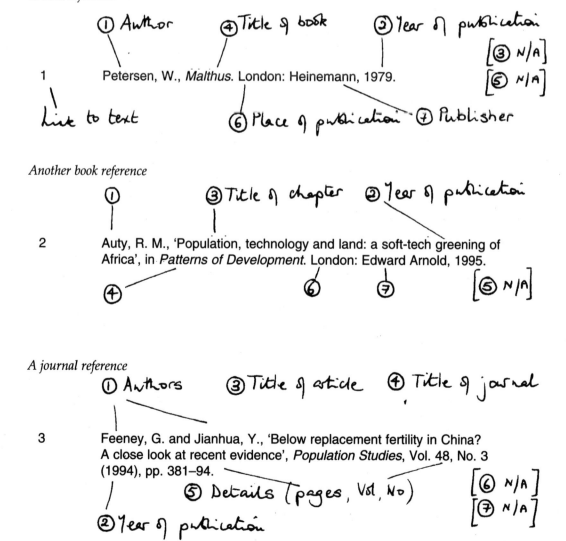

① Author ④ Title of book ② Year of publication [③ N/A] [⑤ N/A]

1   Petersen, W., *Malthus*. London: Heinemann, 1979.

Link to text ⑥ Place of publication ⑦ Publisher

Another book reference

① ③ Title of chapter ② Year of publication

2   Auty, R. M., 'Population, technology and land: a soft-tech greening of Africa', in *Patterns of Development*. London: Edward Arnold, 1995.

④ ⑥ ⑦ [⑤ N/A]

A journal reference

① Authors ③ Title of article ④ Title of journal

3   Feeney, G. and Jianhua, Y., 'Below replacement fertility in China? A close look at recent evidence', *Population Studies*, Vol. 48, No. 3 (1994), pp. 381–94.

② Year of publication ⑤ Details (pages, Vol, No) [⑥ N/A] [⑦ N/A]

You may need to check the specific conventions for how to list publications that differ in some way from the examples here: several authors, newspaper articles, several articles published by the same author in the same year. There is nothing complicated about it: find an example and copy it.

Activity: A bibliography for this student guide

Below (in a random order) are the details of books referred to or consulted in the process of researching this student guide (and some others that may be of interest). Recast them to follow the Harvard system for referencing. The correct bibliography is at the end of the guide.

Derek Rowntree, Learn How to Study, 1970 Macdonald, London

C. Miller and K Swift The Handbook of non-sexist writing for writers, editors and speakers. Women's Press, London 1981

Kate Williams, Study Skills, Macmillan Education Ltd, London, 1989

Diagnosing Dyslexia A Guide to the Assessment of Adults with Specific Learning Difficulties by Cynthia Klein, published by ALBSU, London, 1993

The Complete Plain Words by Sir Ernest Gowers, revised by Sir Bruce Fraser, Harmondsworth, Penguin Books, 2nd edition, 1987

George Orwell, (1946) Politics and the English Language in The Collected Essays, Journalism and Letters of George Orwell Vol 4, Penguin, Harmondsworth, 1970.

References and bibliographies have a purpose central to the academic process: to enable you to move comfortably through the ideas put forward by other writers, to refer to them and comment on them – and to show others the pathway you have taken.

This should explain the carrot and stick approach to referencing and citations used by most higher education institutions. On the one hand they want to encourage good academic practice; on the other they need to ensure that plagiarism is detected and penalized. Plagiarism is when you appear to be passing off other people's thoughts and writing as if they are your own – in effect, copying out chunks of writing without comment, analysis or acknowledgement. This is obviously bad practice, not least because you are not learning or thinking for yourself.

10 Developing your style

Style is not something to worry about. Your style takes shape as you work to find the best form for what you have to say.

This student guide, like the others in the series, is designed as a practical response to the key questions you need to ask before you set out on any writing task. These questions should now be in sharper focus:

- **What** exactly do I have to produce? What content? What form?

- **Why** am I writing this? What do I want to achieve through it?

- **Who** is it for? What are the needs and expectations of my audience?

The answers to these questions lead directly to questions of style. These are the questions to which Gowers (quoted in Section 2.1) directed his readers:

Before you begin to write make sure that you:

YOU MUST KNOW:

- *your subject*

- *your reason for writing*

- *your reader.*

a)   have a clear understanding of your subject

b)   know why you are writing – what does your correspondent want to know and why does he want to know it?

c)   adapt your style and the content of the letter or minute to suit your correspondent's needs and their present knowledge of the subject.

YOU MUST BE:

- *clear*

- *simple and brief*

- *accurate and complete*

- *polite and human.*

You arrive at a style by working to make the bridge between yourself and your reader as smooth as possible. Good writing may seem to have no style: it is just communication between the writer and reader through the words on the page. For how to do this, the advice of George Orwell (1946) is as brilliant as ever:

---

i)   Never use a metaphor, simile or other figure of speech which you are used to seeing in print.

ii)   Never use a long word where a short one will do.

iii) If it is possible to cut a word out, always cut it out.

iv) Never use the passive where you can use the active.

v)   Never use a foreign phrase, a scientific word or a jargon word if you can think of an everyday English equivalent.

vi) Break any of these rules sooner than say anything outright barbarous.

Your motivation to act on Orwell's advice may be boosted by seeing your own and other people's writing analysed objectively, using quantifiable methods. See what you think of the approaches below.

10.1 The FOG index

This is an entertaining way of evaluating the difficulty of a piece of writing – your own, or someone else's.

Activity

1   Take an extract of at least 100 words from the text you are trying to read, or have written. Stop at the end of a sentence. As an example, use the extract from Richard Auty in Section 9.3 above: 'It is clear . . . stability.'

2   Find the average number of words per sentence. Divide the total number of words by the number of sentences.

104 (words) – 3 (sentences)

Average number of words per sentence 34.66

3   Count the number of words with three or more syllables per 100 words. Don't count

- words starting with capital letters

- combinations of short, easy words, e.g., logbook

- verbs made into three syllables by adding 'ed' or 'es'.

Number of words over three syllables . . . 19

4   Add the numbers together:

        Total   53.66

5   Multiply your total by 0.4 and you now have your FOG index   53.66 x 0.4 = 21.46

Interpret your results as follows:

5 . . .	Easy
7 or 8 . . .	Standard
9 to 11 . . .	Fairly difficult
12 to 15 . . .	Difficult
17 + . . .	No wonder you were having problems. . .!

The first paragraph of Chapter 3 ('You know . . . phasing') has a FOG index of 14.1.

You may or may not be convinced that this is an accurate reflection of the difficulty of the passages. It does, however, focus attention on the key aspects of writing that help or hinder the reader: length of sentences and length of words.

Activity

1   Try out the FOG index on extracts from a range of sources – the extracts in the appendix, for example.

2   Take a passage with a high FOG index score and see how you can lower the score by editing the piece in the light of Orwell's advice: 'Never use a long word where a short one will do', and by rewriting to shorten sentences.

10.2 Using 'Grammatik'

The major software producers have developed various forms of grammar checkers, which, until recently, have been of limited use. At the time of going to press, 'Grammatik', integrated into Microsoft wordprocessing software (in WordPerfect 5.2 for Windows, and WordPerfect 6, for example) is now a useful aid to writing. You may find it helpful – entertaining as well as instructive – to play with one of these programs.

The key point about 'Grammatik' is that is makes you look at writing from an objective and technical point of view. In doing so, you find yourself becoming involved in a dialogue about the skills and processes of writing. Below are some of the points I like about the program.

- It's a machine – you can't be offended.

- You identify objective measurements of language and comparative measurements of different types of standard texts, and can see for yourself how different styles work.

- You can set it at different levels and for different styles.

- It is helpful and polite to you as a user: 'You are making your reader's task more difficult here by. . .'

- In commenting on how you put words together, it uses grammar as the natural language for the task. You soon pick up what it means.

- You can ask for explanations and illustrations of terms you don't understand. It will give you a quick run-down on pronouns or adverbs, for example, if you ask.

- It shows you extracts from a range of good source texts for further advice. Gowers is one of them.

- You can control the process, and opt in and out when you want to.

It's well worth trying, and if you are aware that you have a particular problem, such as a tendency to write long sentences, it could be a useful teacher.

10.3 Non-sexist writing

One aspect of Gowers's writing roots him firmly in the society of his time: the use of 'he' to describe both writer and reader. Does it matter if 'he' continues to be used today as a shorthand for all readers and writers? I would argue that it does. If language has the power to shape thought as well as to express it, sexist and biased language betrays and perpetuates prejudice and false assumptions. A non-sexist writing style reflects contemporary society and ensures that you do not implicitly exclude a large portion of readers from your audience by appearing to assume that your reader is male, even – especially – in the traditionally male arenas.

The search to find alternatives to the universal 'he' has, however, led to some clumsy and intrusive constructions. Here are some options that should enable you to keep your writing clear, simple and correct.

Jobs and roles

- Where there is an established neutral term, use it: senior house officer (SHO) (not *houseman*); police officer (not *policeman* or *WPC*); laboratory technician; chair (not *chairman*); parent (not *mother*, where appropriate).

- Where the term is less well established, consider the options: *dustman / refuse collector; foreman / leader, coordinator, convenor.*

- Be aware of outdated assumptions about occupations: *the nurse . . . he; the doctor . . . she;* both are as likely as the reverse.

Pronouns

This is a trickier area, because attempts to be non-sexist can result in some stodgy prose. Below are some strategies to try.

1   Address the reader directly as 'you'.

Most of this guide is written in this style, partly to avoid the leaden repetition of s/he, he or she, she or he, his/her and so on, and partly to make a direct link with the reader. This is useful for instructions, forms, manuals, and other forms of writing that require the reader to interact directly with the text.

2   Use plural forms.

There are plenty of examples of this construction in this guide. See, for example, the short paragraph 'In the end . . . in their way' further down this page.

3   Use 'he or she'.

Save this rather heavy construction for when you want to focus on the individual. You can use the less expected 'she or he' if you want to be more assertive.

4   Be specific.

Use the correct pronoun ('he' or 'she') when you are discussing a known or identifiable individual. When you are discussing an individual in a general way, use 'she' and 'he' interchangeably, and, again, sparingly.

5   Refer to the person's role.

The tutor, the student, the reader, the writer: the role is what matters, not the gender of the person.

6   Use 'they', 'their'.

This is neater than 'he or she', 'his or her', especially when it is repeated several times. This construction will attract flak from some quarters. In mixing the singular and plural, it goes against received wisdom on grammar, although it is also argued that this construction has a worthy historical pedigree (Miller and Swift, 1981). Several major publishing houses in the UK now view this as an acceptable construction where all other possibilities (see above) are inappropriate. Again, use it sparingly!

In the end, your work must read well, convey your meaning clearly to your readers, and not place unnecessary distractions in their way. (Note the use of the plural here; see 2 above.)

> ### Activity
>
> I have used all the constructions listed above in this text.
>
> *   Find examples of each.
>
> *   Do these strategies work? If you find any phrases that place obstacles in your way as a reader, they need rewriting. Answers on a postcard, please!

In this, as in all aspects of writing, you come back to the key questions.

*   **How do you write?**

This guide has given all sorts of details and advice, but this is only useful after you have reached some conclusions about the three strategic questions.

*   **What are you writing?** Your subject, as Gowers put it.

*   **Why are you writing?** Your reason.

*   **Who are you writing for?** Your reader.

Your answers to these questions will guide you to the simple words and structures that will best convey your meaning – if you work at it.

Good luck!

Appendix

These extracts are here as samples of the sorts of things you may have to read. They are used as the basis for a number of activities in this guide.

A

Just possibly, after two years of bitter fighting, peace may soon start spreading faster than war. NATO threats, helped by some crafty Russian diplomacy, have removed Serb guns from Sarajevo. A ceasefire around the city is holding. There are hopes of ending the fierce Bosnian–Croat fighting in central Bosnia, of re-opening Serb-ringed Tuzla airport to UN relief flights, and of relieving the plight of half a dozen more battered and beseiged Bosnian towns. If all this could be done, the outside world would be a long way towards achieving its minimum aim in Bosnia: to quell the fighting and thus limit the carnage. Yet only a negotiated settlement can truly end this brutal war. The breakthrough in Sarajevo has created the opportunity for a wider peace. But it has not made it any easier – it may even be trickier – to get from here to there.

B

If we place one end of a metal rod in a flame and hold the other end, the end we are holding gets hotter and hotter, even though it is not in direct contact with the flame. Heat reaches the cooler end by conduction through the material of the rod. Microscopically, the molecules at the hot end increase the energy of their vibrations as the temperature increases. They then interact with their more slowly moving neighbors farther from the flame; they share some of their energy with these neighbors, who in turn pass it on to those still further from the flame. Thus energy associated with thermal motion is passed along from one molecule to the next, from the hotter end to the cooler, while each individual molecule remains at its original position.

C

In the present paper I draw on a detailed study of social change in a community which has experienced dramatic transitions in both education and fertility limitation within the lifetimes of its members. Previous theories that link education to fertility are divided between those which emphasize decision-makers' own schooling and those which emphasize the schooling of decision-makers' children. In the paper I present an empirical analysis which compares the influence of schooling experiences of various family members on fertility preferences and fertility limitation behaviour. The results show that children's education is an important determinant of parents' decisions to limit fertility during this transition.

D

Transmutation was, of course, an age-old dream. But to men like me, with a theoretical bent of mind, what was most exciting about the 1930s was that there began to open up the evolution of nature. I must explain that phrase. I began here by talking about the day of Creation, and I will do that again. Where shall I start? Archbishop James Ussher of Armagh, a long time ago, about 1650, said that the universe was created in 4004 BC. Armed as he was with dogma and ignorance, he brooked no rebuttal. He or another cleric knew the year, the date, the day of the week, the hour, which fortunately I have forgotten. But the puzzle of the age of the world remained, and remained a paradox, well into the 1900s: because it was then clear that the earth was many, many millions of years old, we could not conceive where the energy came from in the sun and the stars to keep them going so long. By then we had Einstein's equations, of course, which showed that the loss of matter would produce energy. But how was the matter rearranged?

E

```
Work in pairs. Record your results in the results section at
the back of this booklet and get it signed off by one of the
demonstrators when the tables are filled in with your data on
the day of each practical. Demonstrators will only sign the
results once they have been discussed. So do not throw away
your data before discussing your results with a demonstrator.
```

F

The 1947 Town and Country Planning Act imposed compulsory planning duty on local authorities for the first time. Local authorities were given far-reaching powers to control, propose and implement development and land use policies. The inner cities, with their inherent social, economic and physical problems, provided an ideal opportunity for local authority planners to employ these powers. In this essay I will examine the overall effects of this public sector-led renewal in the inner city area.

G

Conclusions

Stratification of the labour market has been identified as an explanation of the development and persistence of low paid sectors in the economy and of the prominence in these sectors of certain categories of workers. In addition to the processes identified by dual and radical theories, workers themselves have contributed to segmentation. A further crucial point to note is that levels of job security and earnings in the two sectors are interdependent; the growth or decline of one sector is bound to affect conditions in the other.

Extract	Source	Audience	
A	Leader in a weekly periodical: 'A Bosnian beginning', *The Economist,* 26 February 1994, p. 18.	Self-selecting general public, with serious interest in understanding current political events.	
B	Physics textbook: Sears et al. (1987), 'Mechanisms of Heat Transfer', *University Physics,* 7th edn. Reading, MA: Addison Wesley, p. 374.	Learners of a specialist subject.	
C	Abstract of a research paper (first published in USA): Axinn, William G. (1993), 'The Effects of Children's Schooling on Fertility Limitation', *Population Studies*, Vol. 47, pp. 481–93.	Students and lecturers in related disciplines worldwide – a comparatively small and specialist group.	
D	Popular science book: Bronowski, J. (1973), *The Ascent of Man.* London: BBC, p. 343.	A self-selecting group of the general public.	
E	Instructions to students.	Science students on a particular course.	
F	Introduction of an undergraduate essay.	Tutor, possibly an examiner/ moderator, or fellow students.	
G	Course handbook on 'Human Resource Management'.	Students new to the subject.	

Evidence	Purpose
Content: summary of recent developments, used to build a structured argument. **Style:** tone of equality with reader (relaxed language: 'crafty', 'trickier').	To engage reader in long-term issues, beyond daily reportage; to persuade reader of the periodical's own assessment of current and future events; to entertain(?): this may be light reading for some readers.
Content: explanation of process. **Style:** direct ('we'), simple tone and language; simple sentence structure. Close sequential links from one sentence to the next.	To inform; to teach essential processes and principles.
Content: summary of results of research. **Style:** personal presentation, a written equivalent to presenting a paper at a conference. Appropriately simple sentence structure and language.	To inform; to share original research with fellow academics and students.
Content: a personal and accessible account of the history of scientific enquiry. **Style:** direct personal style, explaining in simple language.	To engage non-specialists in scientific thinking; to inform and educate through explaining the history of thought and enquiry.
Content: what to do. **Style:** direct definite (perhaps rather abrupt?) using imperative (do this!) and short sentences.	To instruct students to complete practicals in a specific way to meet requirements of the tutor and the course.
Content: overview of key measures, the effects of which will be the subject matter of the essay. **Style:** simple sentence structure, straightforward language.	To demonstrate knowledge and understanding of key measures; to direct reader to specific subject matter of essay.
Content: outline of key terms and concepts. **Style:** a 'teaching' tone – 'a further point to note . . .'.	To introduce students to the language and concepts they will encounter in their subject.

Bibliography

Gowers, Ernest (1987). *The Complete Plain Words*, 2nd edn, rev. Bruce Fraser. Harmondsworth, Penguin.

Klein, Cynthia (1993). *Diagnosing Dyslexia: A Guide to the Assessment of Adults with Specific Learning Difficulties*. London, ALBSU.

Miller, C. and Swift, K. (1981). *The Handbook of Non-Sexist Writing for Writers, Editors and Speakers*. London, Women's Press.

Orwell, George ([1946] 1970). 'Politics and the English Language', in *The Collected Essays, Journalism and Letters of George Orwell*, vol. 4. Harmondsworth, Penguin.

Rowntree, Derek (1970). *Learn How to Study*. London, Macdonald.

Williams, Kate (1989). *Study Skills*. London, Macmillan Education.

Other publications available from **The Oxford Centre for Staff Development**

TEACHING MORE STUDENTS
1 Problems and course design strategies
2 Lecturing to more students
3 Discussion with more students
4 Assessing more students
5 Independent learning with more students
6 Supporting more students
Video: Teaching More Students

COURSE DESIGN FOR RESOURCE BASED LEARNING
Course Design for Resource Based Learning in Social Science
Course Design for Resource Based Learning in Education
Course Design for Resource Based Learning in Technology
Course Design for Resource Based Learning in Accountancy
Course Design for Resource Based Learning in Built Environment
Course Design for Resource Based Learning in Art and Design
Course Design for Resource Based Learning in Business
Course Design for Resource Based Learning in Humanities
Course Design for Resource Based Learning in Science
Institutional Support for Resource Based Learning

LEARNING IN TEAMS SERIES
Learning in Teams: A Student Guide
Learning in Teams: A Student Manual
Learning in Teams: A Tutor Guide

DEVELOPING WRITING SERIES
Essential Writing Skills
Using Data
Writing Reports
Scientific & Technical Writing
Essay Writing
Tutor Manual

LEARNING TO TEACH SERIES
Running Tutorials and Seminars
Making Presentations
Assessing Students' Work
Powerful Ideas in Teaching and Learning

DEVELOPING STUDENTS' TRANSFERABLE SKILLS

STRATEGIES FOR DIVERSIFYING ASSESSMENT

BEING AN EFFECTIVE ACADEMIC

ASSESSING STUDENT CENTRED COURSES

IMPROVING STUDENT LEARNING – THEORY AND PRACTICE

IMPROVING STUDENT LEARNING – THROUGH ASSESSMENT AND EVALUATION

OTHER TITLES IN THE DEVELOPING WRITING SERIES

Essential Writing Skills
Using Data
Writing Reports
Scientific & Technical Writing
Essay Writing
Tutor Manual